BEAUTY THERAPY

Withdrawn

LEVEL 1

Francesca Gould

Nelson Thornes

Published in 2011 by:
Nelson Thornes Ltd
Delta Place
27 Bath Road
CHELTENHAM
GL53 7TH
United Kingdom

11 12 13 14 15 / 10 9 8 7 6 5 4 3 2 1

A catalogue record for this book is available from the British Library

ISBN 978 1 4085 0887 9

Cover photographs: Valua Vitaly/iStockphoto (eye with orange make-up); Zack Blanton/iStockphoto (eye sketch)

Page make-up by Pantek Arts Ltd, Maidstone

Printed and bound in Spain by GraphyCems

Photo acknowledgements

Page 1 Fotolia; page 15 Fotolia; page 18 Ellisons (wax pot, tweezers, nail file, wax strips, hoof stick, buffer, and foot file), BaByliss (Pro Satin Smooth foot spa), REM (facial steamer), Dermalogica (cleanser); page 24 Instant Art; page 26 iStockphoto; page 27 Martin Sookias; page 36 Fotolia; page 49 iStockphoto; page 62 iStockphoto; page 63 iStockphoto; page 86 iStockphoto; page 97 Fotolia; page 100 Martin Sookias.

Contents

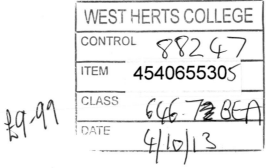

Introduction

Welcome to the Level 1 Beauty Therapy Course Companion. It is a companion to support you throughout your course and record your progress.

This workbook-style book is designed to be used alongside **any** student book you are using. It is packed full of activities for you to complete in order to check your knowledge and reinforce the essential skills you need for this qualification.

Features of the Course Companion are:

Unit opener – this page contains a brief introduction to each unit along with the learning objectives you need to achieve.

Key knowledge – the underpinning knowledge you must know is summarised at the beginning of each unit.

Activities – a wide variety of learning activities are provided for you to complete in Companion book. Each activity is linked to one of the Personal, Learning and Thinking Skills to help you practise these fundamental skills:

 – Reflective Learner   – Self Manager

 – Creative Thinker   – Independent Enquirer

 – Teamworker   – Effective Participator

You will also notice additional icons that appear on different activities, which link to the following core skills:

 – Literacy

 – Numeracy

 – ICT

Key terms – during your course you'll come across new words or new terms that you may not have heard before, so definitions for these have been provided.

Your questions answered – your expert author, Francesca Gould, answers some of the burning questions you may have as you work through the units.

Quick Quiz – at the end of each unit you will find a multiple choice quiz. Answering these will check that you have fully understood what you have learned.

Good luck!

UNIT G20

Ensure responsibility for actions to reduce risks to health and safety

This unit provides you with the knowledge, understanding and skills to be responsible for health and safety in the workplace. Health and safety must be taken very seriously by all employees to ensure that no one becomes injured or harmed in any way. Therapists should be continually risk assessing, which means noticing any potential risks such as a trailing lead, which could cause someone to trip over and become injured.

You will need to be able to:
- identify the hazards and evaluate the risks in the workplace
- reduce the risks to health and safety in the workplace
- understand how to reduce risks to health and safety in the workplace.

Key knowledge

- ✿ Health and safety laws
- ✿ Health and safety terms
- ✿ How to keep a working environment safe for everyone
- ✿ How to maintain hygiene in the work environment
- ✿ How to clean tools and equipment
- ✿ What is meant by a hazard
- ✿ Common skin conditions
- ✿ The basics of first-aid treatment
- ✿ Different types of fire extinguishers
- ✿ What is meant by an allergic reaction

Hazards and errors

key term

Hazard a situation that may be dangerous and has the potential to cause harm.

ACTIVITY

There are numerous health and safety issues in this salon. How many **hazards** or errors can you find in the treatment room? Circle each hazard in the picture.

While working in a salon, you should be continually looking for any potential hazards that could cause harm and create a dangerous situation. You may be able to think of other hazards.

Legislation definitions

ACTIVITY

Match the legislation with the correct definition.

RIDDOR	This Act ensures that job applicants are not discriminated against because of their sex, race or marital status.
Manual Handling Operations Regulations	Staff must know what to do in the event of a fire or emergency and the place of work must have fire exits that are clearly labelled.
Control of Substances Hazardous to Health	This legislation states that employers should provide adequate training regarding lifting, carrying and handling techniques if necessary.
Cosmetic Products (Safety) Regulations	Accidents that occur at work must be entered into an accident book.
The Sex Discrimination Act and the Race Relations Act	This legislation covers substances that are hazardous to health and could cause ill health.
Fire Precautions Act	This Act covers all aspects of health, safety and welfare at work.
Health and Safety at Work Act	These require that cosmetics and toiletries are tested and safe for use.

Health and safety wordsearch

ACTIVITY

Find the following words in the wordsearch below and put a circle around each.

E	A	C	T	E	G	T	O	S	C	I	F	O	I	S	H	L	T	S	E
R	N	F	E	L	I	O	I	U	D	L	U	E	R	R	N	S	D	I	H
U	I	O	N	L	O	S	R	L	A	E	E	E	S	S	O	I	S	H	A
A	B	T	I	N	R	L	K	M	H	S	N	O	D	I	I	D	S	N	D
U	E	N	B	T	T	C	M	C	L	R	I	A	E	N	T	O	D	O	V
L	R	E	A	F	A	A	H	T	I	B	O	A	S	I	C	I	O	I	I
G	A	M	C	S	B	C	O	S	S	A	I	U	I	N	E	L	N	T	R
V	C	S	T	L	S	D	I	A	T	S	R	I	F	S	F	I	E	A	U
O	C	S	E	G	N	I	L	D	N	A	H	L	A	U	N	A	M	L	S
O	I	E	L	C	S	O	N	O	N	N	S	T	E	R	I	L	I	S	E
A	D	S	O	H	U	I	I	C	I	I	E	R	S	I	S	I	I	I	S
R	E	S	I	L	I	R	E	T	S	D	A	E	B	S	S	A	L	G	E
C	N	A	V	S	B	G	I	V	C	O	R	R	S	K	O	N	F	E	H
S	T	K	A	A	C	A	L	T	A	E	A	A	T	S	R	T	S	L	L
R	B	S	R	E	C	L	C	R	Y	L	F	V	Z	N	C	K	A	I	I
N	O	I	T	C	A	A	R	T	N	O	C	N	I	A	O	I	A	R	T
N	O	R	L	C	H	Y	G	I	E	N	E	O	I	A	H	C	A	A	O
R	K	T	U	I	A	I	L	N	I	R	S	C	T	S	N	R	I	C	A
O	I	B	E	R	T	L	I	H	L	C	I	E	I	U	I	E	R	L	E
H	T	C	I	A	L	B	I	A	I	C	U	A	D	I	A	D	H	U	A

accident book
autoclave
bacteria
contra-action
contra-indication
COSHH
cross-infection
disinfection
first aid
flammable
flood
glass bead steriliser
hazard
hygiene
insurance
legislation
manual handling
RIDDOR
risk
risk assessment
sanitise
security
sterilise
ultraviolet cabinet
viruses

ACTIVITY

Choose ten terms from the wordsearch task above and research their definitions.

1.

2.

3.

4.

5.

6.

7.

8.

9.

10.

Spotting hazardous situations

ACTIVITY

Therapists should be continually assessing whether anything in the workplace could be potentially harmful to a person and, by this assessment, reducing the likelihood of accidents occurring. If a salon is held responsible for someone being injured in the workplace, the salon may be sued and could lose its reputation as a professional salon. Write about the following hazardous situations shown in each picture.

Think about what may have caused the situation and how it could have been prevented. Who do you think is responsible and what legislation (laws) has been broken. What could happen to the people involved and the salon as a result of the accident?

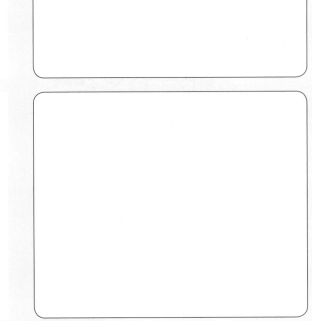

Which legislation am I?

ACTIVITY

You should be aware of important laws relating to working as a beauty therapist. Match the terms in the bubbles with the correct description in the following list:

A I ensure that a workplace has a well-stocked first-aid kit.

Control of Substances Hazardous to Health Regulations 2002

B I ensure that employers control people's exposure to hazardous substances in the workplace.

Environmental Protection Act 1990

C I make certain that employers take out insurance in case of claims made by an employee who suffers an injury or illness as the result of negligence by the employer or another employee.

The Trade Descriptions Act 1968 and 1972

D I cover all aspects of health, safety and welfare at work.

Health and Safety (First Aid) Regulations 1981

E I ensure that fire exits are clearly marked and are not obstructed.

Electricity at Work Regulations 1990

F I state that it is a crime to describe goods falsely and to sell, or offer for sale, goods that have false claims made about them.

Fire Precautions Act 1971

G I state that every electrical appliance at work must be regularly inspected and tested to ensure it is safe for use.

Health and Safety at Work Act 1974

H I ensure that hazardous substances are disposed of correctly so that they do not cause harm to the environment.

Employers' Liability (Compulsory Insurance) Act 1969

These laws are put in place to ensure everyone's safety and also to ensure fair trading.

Health and safety crossword

 ACTIVITY

Answer the clues to complete the crossword.

Across

3. A condition that makes a client unsuitable for treatment (6,10)
6. These tiny mites burrow into the epidermis causing an itchy rash (7)
8. A fire extinguisher that is colour-coded black contains this gas (6, 7)
9. These germs can cause infection within the body (8)
11. A side-effect of a treatment that may happen during or after the treatment (6, 6)
13. The complete destruction of bacteria and their spores (13)
15. This is used to smother a small fire or if a person's clothing is on fire (4, 7)
16. Something that has the potential to cause harm (6)
17. A substance that can easily catch fire (9)

Down

1. A small, electrically heated container that contains glass beads that heat up and help to sterilise small objects such as tweezers (5, 4, 10)
2. Disinfectants that are used specifically on the skin (11)
4. Passing germs from one person to another (5, 9)
5. This fungal infection commonly affects the foot (8, 4)
7. The main risk associated with unsafe electrical equipment (8, 5)
10. A viral infection that commonly features blisters around the mouth (4, 4)
12. A piece of equipment that is highly effective for sterilising items (9)
14. A fire extinguisher that is colour-coded red contains this substance (5)

Legislation and insurance

ACTIVITY

Look at the list and decide which is **legislation** and which are types of insurance. Insert the correct answer under each heading.

Legislation	Insurance

Data Protection Act
Health and Safety at Work Act
Employers' Liability
Fire Precaution Act
Public Liability
Treatment Liability
Control of Substances Hazardous to Health

All salons should have insurance policies to cover them in case they are sued either by a customer or an employee.

Health and safety word hunt

ACTIVITY

Look at the clues below and write the correct answer using the letters from each grid. Remember, you might not have to use all of the letters – some may be red herrings!

1. Refers to any procedures undertaken in the salon to remove dirt and reduce the risk of infection

T	I	B	A
I	N	A	S
S	C	S	N
A	E	I	O

2. Sterilising equipment in which water is boiled, under pressure, to sterilise items such as tweezers

G	O	P	B
T	A	C	L
S	U	E	A
V	D	V	W

3. Tiny organisms that can be harmful (pathogenic) and cause infection

A	N	I	I
A	T	C	O
I	E	A	S
R	L	F	B

4. A cabinet that is used to sanitise small items of equipment

U	I	B	A
A	R	T	C
V	U	L	T
I	O	L	E

5. The transfer of infection through personal contact or indirectly through contact with a contaminated item

O	R	I	O
S	C	T	N
I	S	C	O
N	F	E	W

6. Small parasites that lay eggs on the hair and puncture the skin and suck blood

H	R	E	O
S	E	C	N
I	A	D	L
D	F	O	W

7. A viral infection that affects the liver and includes types A, B and C

J	S	I	O
P	I	T	N
I	T	A	O
N	P	E	H

8. Substance that can be applied to the skin and prevents the growth of bacteria and infection of wounds

A	I	T	B
T	N	C	I
P	E	S	M
C	E	G	L

Hazardous and non-hazardous situations

ACTIVITY

Look at the list of situations. Decide which are hazardous and non-hazardous and insert each into the correct box.

key term

Legislation a law or a body of laws.

Hazardous	Non-hazardous

Broken wax pot
Loose tile on the floor
Magazines on a reception desk
Electrical flex trailing across the trolley
Wax strips placed onto a trolley
Therapist wearing high heels
Puddle of water on the floor
Therapist wearing white overall
Blocked fire exit

The list contains only a few hazardous situations. You can probably think of lots more.

First-aid treatments

 ACTIVITY

Decide the correct first-aid treatment and effect for each problem and enter the correct answer into each box.

First-aid treatments:
Hold under cold running water.
Apply cold compress.
Position person with head between knees.
Lie person down and raise their feet.
Wash it out with clean water poured from a glass or a sterile eye-wash bath.

Effects:
To cool the skin
To reduce pain and swelling
To remove object without damaging the eye
To restore blood flow to the head, as head is in the lowest position and the feet are raised
To restore blood flow to the head

Problem	First-aid treatment	Effect
Dizziness		
Fainting		
Minor burn		
Object in the eye		
Bruises		

If first aid is required, remember to get the help of a qualified first-aider as soon as possible. If the person has had an accident, the details will need to be entered into an accident book.

Firefighting equipment

ACTIVITY

Look at the list of firefighting equipment and insert the correct answer into each box.

A fire extinguisher colour-coded red
A fire extinguisher colour-coded blue
A fire blanket
A fire extinguisher colour-coded black
A fire extinguisher colour-coded cream

Fire safety item	Description
	Contains water. Used for paper, wood, textiles, etc. but not for electrical fires.
	Contains dry powder. Used for flammable liquids and electrical fires.
	Contains foam. Used for flammable liquids but not electrical fires.
	Contains carbon dioxide. Used for flammable liquids and electrical fires.
	Used to smother small fires or if a person's clothing is on fire.

People should be trained in the use of fire extinguishers before using them to put out a fire.

Your questions answered ...

What action should I take if I receive a phone call from a client saying I am responsible for an allergic reaction she suffered after receiving a facial treatment?

Firstly, do not panic. If you are working as a beauty therapist, your salon will have the appropriate insurance to cover for these kinds of problems. Many therapists will have taken out their own insurance policies. As a professional, you will have carried out the correct hygiene procedures and given any necessary allergy testing, therefore it is unlikely that you will have caused any harm by being careless. Inform your manager straight away – he or she will probably deal with the issue. Insurance companies will often advise that the client return to the salon so the therapist and manager can observe the problem, and make notes on the client's treatment card. This is why it is important to note information, such as providing an allergy test to a client, onto their card. If required, this can be used as evidence if a client decides to sue the salon.

QUICK QUIZ

1. What is meant by a 'hazard'?
   a. Electrical equipment not being regularly checked
   b. Something that could cause an accident or injury
   c. A cross infection
   d. A contraindication

2. What is meant by 'risk assessment'?
   a. Ensuring the client's belongings are put in a safe place to avoid theft
   b. Checking that all windows and doors are not broken and can be locked
   c. Identifying risks in the workplace that could cause harm to someone
   d. Assessing the safety of all electrical equipment

3. What do the letters COSHH stand for?
   a. Control of Substances Hazardous to Health
   b. Control of Substances Hurtful to Health
   c. Control of Situations Hazardous to Health
   d. Control of Substances Helpful to Health

4. Which of the following types of legislation relate directly to employers and employees maintaining high standards of health and safety?
   a. Consumer Protection Act 1987
   b. Health and Safety at Work Act 1974
   c. RIDDOR
   d. Data Protection Act 1998

5. Which of the following concerns the Environmental Protection Act 1990?
   a. Picking up heavy items
   b. Ensuring that the working environment is hygienic
   c. Ensuring that electrical equipment is checked regularly
   d. The safe disposal of hazardous substances

6. If the Health and Safety at Work Act 1974 is not followed, what could be the result?
   a. The therapist or the salon could be fined
   b. The salon could be closed down
   c. The therapist or salon owner could be imprisoned
   d. All of the above

7. Which Act is concerned with personal information about individuals that is stored on a computer or in an organised paper filing system?
   a. The Consumer Protection Act 1987
   b. RIDDOR 1995
   c. The Local Government Act 1982
   d. The Data Protection Act 1998

8. Which Act is concerned with goods that are falsely described?
   a. Trade Descriptions Act 1968 and 1972
   b. Disability and Equality Act 2010
   c. Data Protection Act 1998
   d. Fire Precautions Act 1971

9. The Employers' Liability Act 1969 covers claims that may result from which of the following?
   a. Any accidents that happen in the salon
   b. Injury to the employer
   c. Injury to an employee (therapist) in the workplace (salon)
   d. Any faulty equipment

10. The symbol for a substance that is an irritant, for instance, to the skin is:
    a. A flame
    b. A skull and cross bones
    c. A large black cross
    d. Exploding objects

UNIT B1

Prepare and maintain salon treatment work areas

This unit is about preparing and maintaining the beauty therapy work area. It covers preparing the work area for waxing, eye treatments, make-up, nail and facial treatments. It deals with setting up materials and equipment for these treatments, maintaining personal appearance and hygiene and obtaining the clients' records.

You will also need to get rid of waste after the treatments, safely store client records, clean the work area and leave it in a suitable condition for the next treatment.

You will need to:
❋ be able to prepare the treatment work areas
❋ be able to maintain the treatment work areas
❋ know about organisational and legal requirements
❋ know how to prepare and maintain the treatment work areas.

Key knowledge

✿ Laws associated with preparing and maintaining salon treatment work areas
✿ Your organisation's (salon's) requirements for setting up a treatment area
✿ The main beauty treatments that are carried out in a salon
✿ Which products and equipment are required for each treatment
✿ The methods of cleaning equipment

Health and safety legal requirements

key term

Germs tiny organisms, such as bacteria, which are capable of causing illness.

ACTIVITY

Write down 10 ways in which you can ensure you act safely and hygienically while working in a salon.

The treatment area and equipment should be kept clean at all times to help prevent the spread of **germs**.

1.

2.

3.

4.

5.

6.

7.

8.

9.

10.

Laws

ACTIVITY

Research legislation (laws) and decide and write down which are related to the following:

Disposal of hazardous waste:

Blocking of fire exits:

Client record cards:

Dealing with hazardous substances, e.g. flammable beauty products:

Using the correct posture when picking up heavy items:

The unprofessional therapist

ACTIVITY

Look at the picture of the therapist. List five ways in which she appears unprofessional.

1.

2.

3.

4.

5.

Which beauty product, equipment or material am I?

ACTIVITY

Look at each picture and name the product, equipment or material.

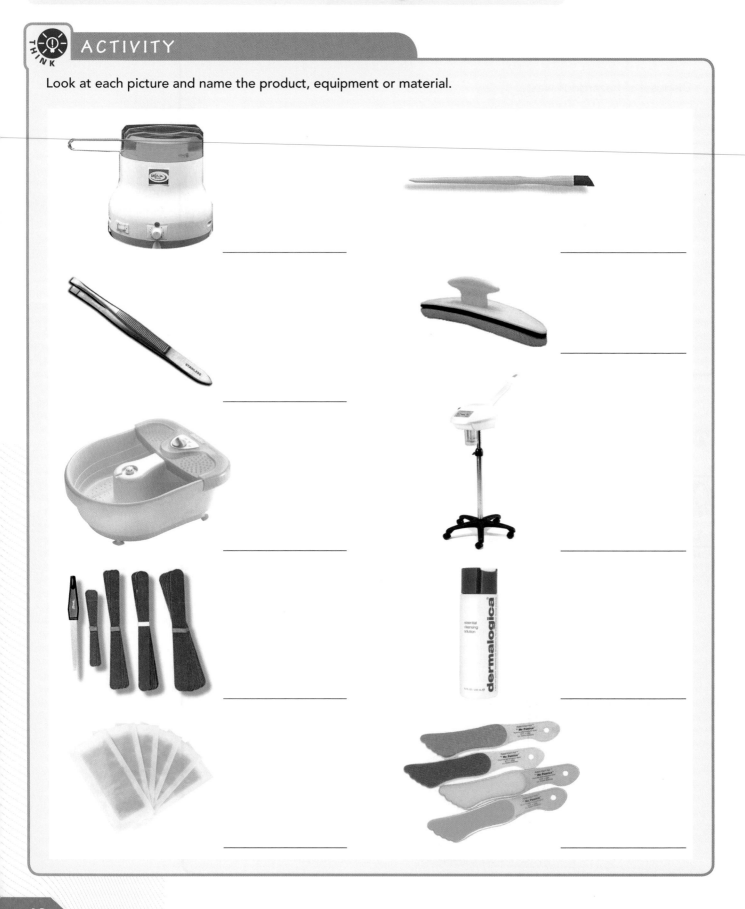

_____

_____

_____

_____

_____

_____

_____

_____

_____

_____

Which beauty treatment am I?

ACTIVITY

Fill in the gaps using the words in bubbles.

waxing   nail extensions   pedicure   facial

make-up   eyelash tint   spa   manicure

1. A _____ treatment includes cleansing, toning and moisturising the skin of the face.

2. A _____ treatment helps to improve the condition of the nails and the skin of the hands.

3. _____ is a method of temporary hair removal.

4. A _____ treatment involves using products such as eyeshadow and lipstick.

5. An _____ treatment involves permanent dyeing of the eyelashes.

6. _____ treatments include hydrotherapy and heat treatments.

7. _____ involve applying artificial nails to the natural nail.

8. A _____ involves treating the feet to help enhance the appearance of the nails and the skin of the feet.

Beauty treatments wordsearch

ACTIVITY

Find the following words in the wordsearch below and put a circle around each.

X	N	F	T	I	I	N	C	N	N	X	T	C	M	S	N
S	P	M	A	N	I	C	U	R	E	A	O	T	L	N	C
P	E	A	R	P	I	E	R	C	I	N	G	A	A	O	R
I	E	S	N	S	P	T	X	I	S	I	I	I	S	I	A
D	P	S	G	T	R	A	W	U	O	C	L	E	E	S	R
T	I	A	A	N	S	L	L	O	A	A	H	P	R	N	B
N	L	G	N	E	I	T	U	F	R	S	I	N	U	E	O
A	A	E	A	M	A	X	L	T	A	B	E	O	C	T	D
E	T	N	I	T	H	S	A	L	E	Y	E	U	I	X	Y
M	I	T	I	A	I	N	P	W	N	E	I	Y	D	E	T
C	O	O	D	E	P	I	L	A	T	I	O	N	E	L	A
E	N	A	O	R	R	C	A	G	Y	A	L	E	P	I	N
L	E	U	A	T	I	D	T	S	S	N	C	O	E	A	N
S	E	H	S	A	L	L	A	U	D	I	V	I	D	N	I
N	T	G	I	P	U	E	K	A	M	G	E	I	M	A	N
P	D	I	I	S	L	U	E	L	A	E	I	E	I	I	G

body tanning
consultation
depilation
ear piercing
epilation
eyebrow tint
eyelash tint
facial
individual lashes

make-up
manicure
massage
nail art
nail extensions
pedicure
spa treatments
strip lashes
waxing

key term

Epilation removal of the whole hair from the skin, including the root.

Which waxing equipment or material am I?

ACTIVITY

Using different coloured pencils, match the equipment and materials to the relevant descriptions by shading the bubbles and description 'key' in corresponding colours.

wax heater	These should be worn to help prevent cross-infection.
spatulas	Items such as tweezers and scissors can be placed into a jar containing this liquid to help keep them clean.
pre-wax lotion	These are used to remove any remaining hairs after treatment.
tweezers	These are usually made of wood and are used to apply wax to the skin.
sanitising solution	This item needs to be turned on about 30 minutes before the client arrives.
wax strips	These may be paper or fabric and are used to remove wax from the skin.
surgical gloves	This is applied after the waxing treatment to help soothe the area.
after-wax lotion	This helps to clean and remove any oil from the area to be waxed.

Beauty tools and equipment

ACTIVITY

Look at the list below. Decide which tools are required for each of the following treatments and place them into the correct box.

Cuticle remover
Emery board
Wax pot
Surgical gloves
After-wax lotion
Strip lashes
Eyelash tint
Mask brush
Steaming
Cleanser

Buffer
Foot file
Wax strips
Wax
Eyeshields
Tint brush
Individual lashes
Moisturiser
Toner

Waxing	Eye treatments

Manicures and pedicures	Facial treatments

Eyelash-tint treatment

ACTIVITY

key term

Barrier cream a substance used to prevent eyelash tint from staining the skin, e.g. petroleum jelly.

Study the list of beauty tools, products and equipment and decide which are required to carry out an eyelash tint. Draw the items onto the trolley.

Lipstick

10 vol. hydrogen peroxide

Exfoliant

Eyelash tint

Eye make-up remover

After-wax lotion

Tinting brush

Buffer

Cotton wool

Barrier cream

Cuticle cream

Top coat

Small glass dish

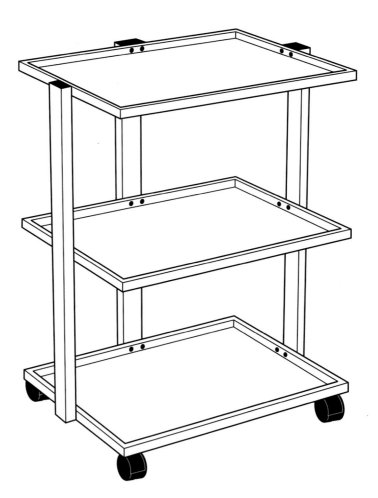

It's important that you neatly prepare a treatment area and that you arrange the products so that they are attractively laid out.

Beauty treatments crossword

  ACTIVITY

Answer the clues to complete the crossword.

Across

4. Often made of wood and is used to apply wax to the skin (7)
8. This is used to help soothe the skin after a waxing treatment (8, 6)
9. Usually carried out twice during a facial treatment (4)
11. Consists of gritty bits and helps to make the nails shiny (7, 5)
12. Given at least 24 hours before treatment in case the client is allergic to any of the products used (7, 4)
13. This item is used to help keep the hair away from the face (8)
14. Includes effleurage and petrissage techniques (7)

Down

1. Helps to prevent staining of the nails and is applied underneath nail polish (8)
2. Helps to soften the skin and often contains **sunscreen** to help protect the skin from the sun's rays (11)
3. This product is mixed with the tint (8, 8)
5. Item which can be used to remove hairs from the skin (8)
6. Helps to prevent staining of the skin while carrying out an eyelash tinting (7, 5)
7. A sponge is often used to apply this make-up product to the face (10)
10. Helps to remove dead skin cells from the skin (10)
11. An eyelash tint colour (5)

key term

Sunscreen a substance that helps protect the skin from the sun's harmful rays

23

I've noticed that there are hazard symbols on certain beauty products. What do they mean?

The main hazard symbols you will come across as a beauty therapist include the following:

 Harmful if breathed in or swallowed. Irritating to the eyes and respiratory system.

 The vapours of these substances will catch fire if they come into contact with a spark or a flame.

 Can cause burns to the skin or eyes. If breathed in can burn the lining of the nose, throat and lungs.

 A substance is **toxic** if breathed in, swallowed or comes in contact with the skin.

key term

Toxic something that can be harmful to health.

Use books and the internet to research more hazard symbols and their meanings.

It's important to understand these types of hazard warnings on products to help prevent anyone becoming harmed due to incorrect handling or use of a product.

QUICK QUIZ

HOW MUCH DO YOU KNOW ABOUT MAINTAINING SALON TREATMENT WORK AREAS?

1. What is the most important reason for wearing gloves during waxing treatment?
   a. To prevent the hands from getting dirty
   b. It helps to prevent the therapist from accidentally scratching the client
   c. It looks professional
   d. It helps to prevent cross-infection

2. After items such as tweezers have been thoroughly cleansed, they may be placed into a jar containing which substance?
   a. Cleanser
   b. Sanitising solution
   c. Acetone
   d. Bleach

3. What is the main reason for using clean towels while providing a treatment?
   a. So they smell nice
   b. It looks professional
   c. To avoid the passing of germs, which could cause infection
   d. Wipes up spillages more easily

4. What is the most important reason for checking that a wax pot is not damaged before use?
   a. It would annoy the therapist if it was damaged
   b. To prevent injury to the client or therapist
   c. In case wax leaks from it and causes loss of profit
   d. If there are loose wires, it doesn't look professional

5. What is the difference between manual and automatic tweezers?
   a. Automatic tweezers remove hairs more quickly than manual ones
   b. Manual tweezers remove more hairs in a shorter space of time than automatic ones
   c. Automatic tweezers are smaller and darker in colour than manual ones
   d. Automatic tweezers are longer and require two hands to work them

6. Which of the following items would be used during an eyelash-tint treatment?
   a. Buffer
   b. Massage cream
   c. Shader
   d. Hydrogen peroxide

7. Which of the following would not be used during a waxing treatment?
   a. Wax strips
   b. Tweezers
   c. Exfoliator
   d. Spatula

8. What is the purpose of an allergy test, also known as a patch test?
   a. To help sell products to a client
   b. To ensure that the client is not allergic to products used during the treatment
   c. To see which make-up colours suit a client
   d. To test the therapist's knowledge of certain products

9. If a tissue contained blood, you would firstly put on gloves but what would you do next?
   a. Flush it down the toilet
   b. Give it to the client
   c. Put into a sealed waste bag
   d. Throw it into a waste paper bin

10. What strength hydrogen peroxide should be added to eyelash and eyebrow tint?
    a. 10 vol
    b. 5 vol
    c. 3 vol
    d. 15 vol

UNIT G3

Contribute to the development of effective working relationships

This unit is about forming good relationships with clients in a way that promotes goodwill and trust, being able to work effectively when supporting your colleagues and using the opportunities for learning that happen within your job role.

You will need to be able to:
* develop effective working relationships with clients and colleagues
* develop self within your job role
* understand the salon's and legal requirements
* understand communication methods
* understand procedures and targets
* understand how to improve your own performance
* understand how to work with others.

Key knowledge

✿ How to work as part of a team
✿ How to work in a professional manner
✿ The code of ethics
✿ The different methods of communication
✿ The salon's procedures regarding working in the salon
✿ What is meant by targets
✿ What action can be taken to improve your work

Code of ethics

 ACTIVITY

When working with clients, you should always consider the **code of ethics**. State five guidelines that relate to the code of ethics and should always be followed.

1.

2.

3.

4.

5.

key term

Code of ethics set of guidelines which help to ensure a beauty therapist behaves professionally while working with clients.

Following these guidelines will help to ensure that you carry out a professional service and therefore will be highly regarded as a beauty therapist.

Developing an effective working relationship

key term

Colleague a person that you work with.

 ACTIVITY

Think about how you would like to be treated by **colleagues** while working in a salon. Make a list of five points.

1.

2.

3.

4.

5.

Remember to treat your colleagues in the same way as you expect to be treated.

Poor service

 ACTIVITY

Working in a small group, choose a couple of students to act out the scenes below. Afterwards, discuss what was wrong with each scene and what should have actually happened.

Scenes

1. A client complains that a lipstick she bought from the salon was of poor quality. The therapist becomes aggressive, folds her arms, frowns and says, 'Well, nobody else has complained and I can see that you have used it.'

2. A client is having a leg wax and says, 'Ooh, that really hurts.' The therapist replies, 'Well, what do you expect, surely you realised it would be painful?'

3. One therapist says to another, 'I am running late for my next client, would you get me a couple of towels?' and the other therapist replies, 'No, you get them yourself, I'm having a break.'

4. A therapist is on the telephone in the reception area. A client comes to the desk. The therapist looks at her and says, 'I'm not sure how long I'm going to be so take a seat over there.'

5. A client demands that she wants an eyelash tint despite not having had an eyelash-tint allergy test. The therapist decides to provide the treatment anyway.

Job roles

 ACTIVITY

When applying for jobs, you will come across various terms. Use books and the internet to research and describe the following terms:

Self management

Be punctual

Give a service attitude

Ability to communicate

Is able to prioritise

Able to work under pressure

Positive attitude

Customer focused

Trade/skills test

Cultural awareness

Personal performance

ACTIVITY

Think about your strengths and weaknesses. Write a brief account of two of your strengths and two of your weaknesses, such as poor organisation. Describe what action you could take to improve any weaknesses.

We all have strengths and weaknesses: maybe you could ask a fellow student to help you with this task. Remember to be respectful and polite when discussing each other's strengths and weaknesses.

Effective working

ACTIVITY

Match each term to its meaning:

Contract of employment	Working with others and supporting them with their roles.
Teamwork	A **legally binding** document which sets out your job description and conditions.
Code of ethics	A particular course of action intended to achieve a result.
Work appraisal	A set of guidelines which a therapist must follow to ensure a professional manner is carried out at all times.
Procedure	Amount of sales which is set by a manager for a certain amount of time.
Sales target	An assessment of your progress at work.

key term

Legally binding an agreement that is enforceable in a court of law.

Negative body language

ACTIVITY

Look at the picture of the therapist and list five ways in which her body language is unprofessional. Also describe what you think each aspect of body language is communicating.

1.

2.

3.

4.

5.

This type of language is very important as most of what we communicate to others is through body language.

Positive body language

ACTIVITY

Describe four ways in which we communicate positively through body language and discuss what is being communicated.

1.

2.

3.

4.

A person showing this kind of body language will seem approachable, friendly and professional.

Work effectively wordsearch

ACTIVITY

Find the following words in the wordsearch:

L	G	P	K	P	E	R	R	K	S	S	A	E	A	T	T	O
R	T	F	L	T	J	E	C	S	M	A	N	A	G	E	R	A
W	E	R	L	S	O	N	R	S	R	A	O	O	R	G	R	T
E	O	S	T	E	B	A	P	P	R	A	I	S	A	L	C	T
A	I	T	G	T	R	D	O	J	W	K	T	N	O	I	S	I
K	A	E	E	E	O	A	O	L	R	N	I	S	I	E	E	T
N	O	O	I	D	L	I	C	O	P	S	T	L	I	I	N	U
E	E	E	C	A	E	E	W	R	A	R	E	L	R	I	T	D
S	C	N	S	R	S	M	O	T	E	S	P	O	K	O	G	E
S	N	O	I	T	A	C	I	N	U	M	M	O	C	C	L	O
E	C	E	U	E	E	O	G	O	O	A	O	P	R	B	T	H
S	I	C	T	D	N	T	R	C	K	O	C	T	I	E	T	A
O	N	O	U	C	H	D	U	K	G	T	E	X	S	N	I	F
C	K	R	R	S	A	T	W	C	C	T	E	O	I	U	I	L
S	E	U	G	A	E	L	L	O	C	L	L	T	R	S	C	G
S	T	E	G	R	A	T	N	T	F	U	S	L	G	M	S	G
S	R	S	M	G	O	A	L	S	C	M	O	L	E	T	N	B

appraisal
attitude
colleagues
communications
competition
customer care
flexible
goals
job roles
manager
organisation
procedures
stock control
strengths
targets
teamwork
trade test
weaknesses

You will need to become familiar with all of these terms.

Your questions answered ...

What would I do if a salon manager wanted me to carry out a treatment I wasn't qualified to do?

Do not carry out job roles you are not qualified to do. You could harm your clients and get into trouble. The Beauty Therapy National Occupation Standards are standards that inform beauty therapists what skills they must be able to carry out on clients and what things they must know and understand. Be honest with your employer from the start to ensure that they know what skills you have. Employers will want to see your beauty certificates and will probably keep a copy of them for insurance purposes.

Use the internet to research National Occupation Standards to find out more.

QUICK QUIZ

1. If you have a disagreement with a work colleague, what action should you take?
   a. Complain about her to your other colleagues to get their opinions
   b. Discuss it with your manager
   c. Discuss it with your colleague and try to sort out the matter in a friendly manner
   d. Ignore him or her for as long as possible

2. A contract of employment is:
   a. a complete list of all the beauty treatments you are required to carry out
   b. an agreement between an employer and employee that details the rights, responsibilities and duties agreed between them
   c. a legal document that discusses the salon's employees' roles and responsibilities
   d. a full job description that discusses hours of work, products used and the pay structure

3. A trade/skills test requested by a beauty employer requires you to:
   a. perform a certain beauty treatment, such as waxing, to show you can competently carry it out
   b. answer a series of multiple-choice questions about beauty treatments and products used
   c. carry out a trial work period in a salon
   d. all of the above

4. A code of ethics:
   a. is a set of rules to ensure professional and appropriate behaviour of an individual
   b. refers to specific **jargon** and language used in a salon
   c. helps to ensure all legal and safety requirements are complied with
   d. is a document you sign when you begin employment.

5. A method of evaluating a person's work performance in a salon is called a:
   a. work apparel
   b. skills appraisal
   c. conduct assessment
   d. work appraisal

key term

Jargon language that is used by a certain group of people, such as beauty therapists.

UNIT B2

Assist with facial skincare treatments

This unit is about assisting with facial treatments. You will need to be able to prepare for treatments by setting up the work area, using consultation techniques, performing a skin analysis and preparing the client. You will also need to be able to assist with facial treatment including cleansing, removing eye make-up, toning, mask application and moisturising. The treatment will also involve checking that the finished effect is to the satisfaction of the senior therapist and the client, and advising the client on aftercare.

To complete this unit, you will need to maintain effective health, safety and hygiene throughout your work. You will also need to maintain your personal appearance and achieve good communication with the client.

You will need to be able to:

✿ use safe and effective methods of working when assisting with facial treatments
✿ consult, plan and prepare for treatments
✿ carry out facial treatments
✿ know organisational and legal requirements
✿ know how to work safely and effectively when assisting with facial treatments
✿ know how to perform client consultation and treatment planning
✿ know the structure of the skin in relation to assisting with facial skincare
✿ know basic facial care products, treatments and aftercare.

Key knowledge

✿ Laws relating to giving a facial treatment
✿ How to label a diagram of the skin and the function of each of the structures
✿ Basic skin conditions and whether they are infectious
✿ How to work safely and effectively
✿ How to prepare a work area for facial treatment
✿ Which products are required for facial treatment and their uses
✿ Factors that can affect the skin's condition and appearance
✿ How to carry out a consultation with a client
✿ Familiarity with a consultation form and a treatment plan
✿ The differences between skin types
✿ Each step of the facial routine
✿ The different types of massage
✿ The main types of **massage mediums**
✿ Awareness of aftercare advice and how often a client should return for further facial treatment

> **key term**
>
> **Massage mediums** substances used to carry out a massage.

The structures of the skin

ACTIVITY

Unscramble the anagrams below to reveal the structures of the skin. Use the answers to label the skin diagram below and give a brief description for each structure.

Bandage loss cue

Snore very sen

Boss dove sell

Suite side soap

Slumec

Primeside

Misred

Airport relic

Candle cringe

Absolute saucy rune

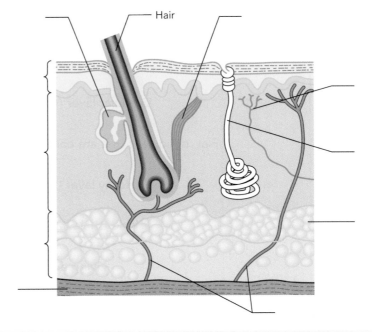

Hair

Understanding the structures of the skin will help you understand how treatments carried out during a facial service affect and benefit the skin.

Epidermis

ACTIVITY

Use different coloured pencils to colour each skin layer in the diagram. Using the same colour that you have used for each layer, circle the correct name of the layer and its description listed below.

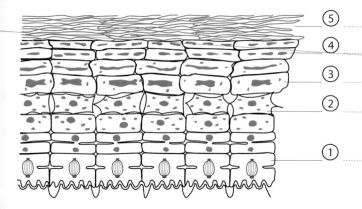

Basal layer (*stratum germinativum*)

Cells are living and interlock by arm-like threads

Found on fingertips, palms of hands and soles of feet

Clear layer (*stratum lucidum*)

Deepest layer in the epidermis

Granular layer (*stratum granulosum*)

Flat, dead cells that are continually shedding from the skin

Horny layer (*stratum corneum*)

Prickle-cell layer (*stratum spinosum*)

Living and dead cells

Skin structures

key term

Vitamin D a vitamin needed by the body to ensure strong and healthy bones.

THINK

ACTIVITY

Match the skin structure to the function. Put the correct answer into each box.

Subcutaneous layer

Capillaries

Vitamin D

Melanin

Eccrine glands

Acid mantle

Collagen fibres

Sensory nerve endings

Arrector pili

Sebaceous glands

Blood flows through them	
Produces a fatty substance called sebum	
Help to give the skin strength	
Produce sweat on the skin's surface	
Mixture of sweat and sebum on the skin	
Situated below the dermis	
Pigment that gives skin its colour	
Make us aware of feelings of pain, touch, heat and cold	
Small muscles that attach to the hair follicles	
Made in the skin due to the action of ultraviolet rays from the sun	

Skin four-in-a-row

 ACTIVITY

This is a game that involves two or more players. The objective of the game is to complete a row of four boxes vertically, horizontally or diagonally. You will need to make photocopies of the two tables.

The table headed 'Skin four-in-a-row (1)' should be placed in front of the players to act as a game board. The table headed 'Skin four-in-a-row (2)' should be cut into cards. All of the cards are shuffled and placed face down. Each player selects a card and reads it aloud. If they answer the question correctly, they may place the card on the correct box on the game board. If they answer incorrectly, they miss a turn. If a question has previously been answered correctly and the box is covered, the card holder misses a turn. The winner is the first person who completes a row of four vertically, horizontally or diagonally.

Skin four-in-a-row (1)

Arrector pili muscle	Sensory nerve	Sebaceous gland	Subcutaneous layer
Epidermis	Basal layer	Melanocytes	Keratin
Blood vessels	Dermis	Horny layer	Acid mantle
Granular layer	Hair	Eccrine gland	Muscle

Skin four-in-a-row (2)

Muscle that contracts hair	Structure that sends messages about our environment to the brain	Produces sebum, which is the skin's natural moisturiser	Adipose tissue (fat) is mostly found in this layer
The top five layers of the skin	Mitosis (cell division) takes place in this layer	Releases melanin, which is a pigment responsible for the colour of our skin and hair	A protein that is found in the skin, hair and nails
Carries oxygen and nutrients that are essential for healthy skin, hair and nails	Contains the papillary and reticular layers. Collagen and elastin can also be found here	Layer of skin that is continually shedding. The cells in this layer are flat and dead	Sweat and sebum mix to form this
Skin layer in which cells begin to die as they fill with granules	Structure found in the hair follicle	Type of sweat gland that is found all over the body	Found between the subcutaneous layer and bone

You can make up your own four-in-a-row game for facial products and treatments.

Skin conditions

 ACTIVITY

Study the skin conditions in books and on the internet and complete the table below.

Skin condition	State if due to bacterial infection, viral infection, fungal infection, parasite or other	Infectious or non-infectious
Eczema		
Psoriasis		
Boils		
Shingles		
Chloasma		
Corns		
Verrucas		
Melanoma		
Styes		
Athlete's foot		
Cold sore		
Vitiligo		
Albinism		
Conjunctivitis		
Scabies		
Rosacea		
Impetigo		
Lentigines		
Naevus		
Freckles		
Ringworm		
Hair lice		
Folliculitis		
Urticaria		
Comedones		
Skin tags		
Acne vulgaris		
Dermatitis		
Milia		
Port wine stain		
Warts		
Allergies		

It's important you know which skin conditions are infectious so that you do not touch them and cross-infect.

What skin condition am I?

ACTIVITY

A I can be due to a bacterial or viral infection. I am **infectious** and cause an eye to become red and irritated.

B I am caused by a virus and am infectious. You will usually find me around the mouth and I will be red and crusty.

C I am also called blackheads and you will often see me as little black dots on the face. I am formed when sebum becomes trapped in a follicle.

D I am not infectious and show myself as red, thickened patches of dry skin. I happen because skin cells are made too quickly in certain areas of the skin.

E I am common during teenage years and am caused by an overproduction of sebum. I appear as red spots and blackheads, and am usually seen on the face, neck and back.

key term

Infectious can pass from one person to another.

Factors that adversely affect the skin

ACTIVITY

Each of the following factors is not beneficial to the skin. Discuss how each affects the skin.

The diet and the consequence on the skin due to lack of nutrients ...

Drinking alcohol ...

Smoking cigarettes ...

Certain medication ...

Ultraviolet light

ACTIVITY

Use books and the internet to research the effects of ultraviolet light on the skin. Discuss what ultraviolet is and what it does to the structure within the skin. Describe how the skin can be protected from it. Try to write about 150 words.

Skin types

ACTIVITY

Match each skin type on the left to its correct definition on the right.

| Normal | This skin type reddens easily when touched and certain substances may irritate it. |

| Oily | This skin type shows areas of dry, normal and oily skin. |

| Dry | This skin type becomes dry as the sebaceous glands become less active with age. The skin may be thin and wrinkles will be present. |

| Sensitive | This skin type shows flaky patches, broken capillaries, a dull colour and/or a rough texture. |

| Combination | This skin type looks healthy, clear and fresh. |

| Mature | Due to excess sebum production, this skin type may look and feel greasy and is more prone to acne and breakouts. |

Understanding a client's skin type can help you to decide the correct products to use on their skin. Usually the forehead, nose and chin are oily – this is known as the T-zone.

Skin ageing

ACTIVITY

Use books and the internet to find out the changes that take place in the face as people age. Discuss what happens to the structures within the skin, its texture, appearance and colour.

Regular facial treatments and following the correct skincare routines at home can help slow down the signs of ageing.

Consultation form

ACTIVITY

In a small group, discuss what information should be included on a consultation from. Then make a list of 12 items of such information.

1.   7.

2.   8.

3.   9.

4.   10.

5.   11.

6.   12.

Treatment plan

ACTIVITY

A treatment plan is essential to ensure that the facial treatment meets with the client's needs. It makes you think about which products would most benefit your client's skin.

Work in pairs to devise a facial treatment plan that contains all the information you would need to provide a professional facial treatment to suit a client with dry skin, and also for a client with an oily skin type.

Client's skincare routine

ACTIVITY

Information about your client's skincare routine will help you to understand how skin problems may have arisen and will also allow you to give them skincare advice to make sure that they look after their skin properly in the future.

In pairs, think of a list of questions you would ask your client to get information about their skincare routine and any factors that may be affecting their skin, such as too much sun exposure.

Safe and effective treatment

ACTIVITY

REFLECT

List ten ways in which the therapist can ensure that the treatment they give is safe and effective.

1.

2.

3.

4.

5.

6.

7.

8.

9.

10.

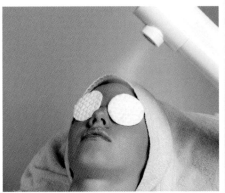

Prepare for treatment

ACTIVITY

Which of the following items would be required for facial treatment? Draw the items onto the trolley.

Cleanser

Eyelash tint

Toner

Mask

Wax strip

Eyeshadow

Lipstick

Bowl of cotton wool

Hoof stick

Moisturiser

Which facial product am I?

ACTIVITY

Match the products in the bubbles with the correct description in the list.

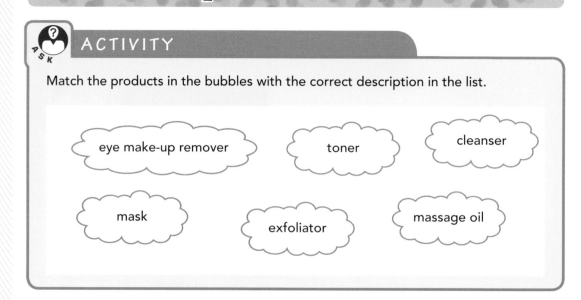

eye make-up remover

toner

cleanser

mask

exfoliator

massage oil

I am often applied to the face with a brush and can be described as 'setting' or 'non-setting'.

I am applied to the skin after it has been cleansed. Sometimes I contain alcohol, which helps to dissolve grease and tighten the skin and which makes pores appear smaller.

I remove dead skin cells from the skin's surface and help it to feel soft and smooth.

I help to get rid of dirt and grime from the skin and am normally used at the beginning of a facial treatment.

I am particularly useful for removing mascara and eyeshadow, especially if I contain oil.

I am often used to carry out a very relaxing part of the facial treatment, which includes movements such as effleurage.

Massage mediums

ACTIVITY

List two mediums (type of products) that can be used for facial massage.

Aromatherapy oils are often included in massage mediums.

key term

Aromatherapy
treatment that involves using oils taken from various plants.

Cleansers

  ACTIVITY

Describe the main difference between cleansers that are produced for dry skin types and those made for oily skin types. Then list five different types of cleanser, e.g. foaming gel cleanser.

1.

2.

3.

4.

5.

Clay masks

 ACTIVITY

List five main clay ingredients used in clay masks and describe the effects of each.

1.

2.

3.

4.

5.

Clay masks are types of setting masks.

Massage movements

ACTIVITY

Use books and the internet to research the following massage movements. Briefly discuss each movement and the effects they have on the face and neck.

Effleurage

Uses of effleurage

Effects of effleurage

Petrissage

Uses of petrissage

Effects of petrissage

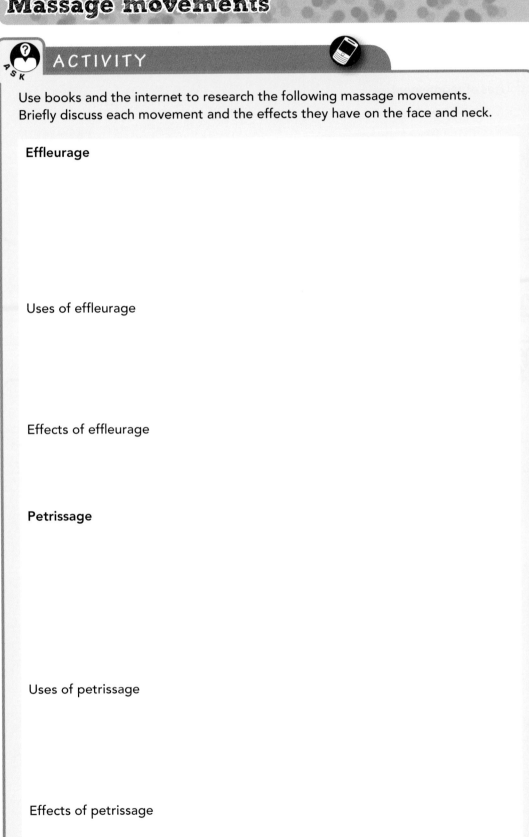

key terms

Effleurage a French word meaning to stroke lightly.

Petrissage a French word meaning to knead.

Tapotement

Uses of tapotement

Effects of tapotement

Treating different skin types

ACTIVITY

In small groups, think about how treatments would differ for the following skin types:

Dry skin

Oily skin

Combination skin

Sensitive skin

Facial treatments – fill in the gaps

ACTIVITY

Look at the list of words below and use them to fill in the gaps.

toner	petrissage	humectant	exfoliant
non-setting	analysis	ultraviolet	sunscreens
pores	cleansing	superficial	masks
complexion	moisturiser	alcohol	

1. A skin _____ may be carried out so that the therapist can decide which products would best suit the client's skin type.

2. There are generally two types of skin cleansing, and these are _____ and deep cleansing.

3. A _____ can be used to help remove the greasy film that remains after cleansing. An astringent effect occurs if it contains _____ and so the skin is temporarily tightened, making the _____ appear smaller.

4. An _____ removes dead skin cells from the skin's surface, helping it to feel soft and smooth. It also brightens up the _____ .

5. A relaxing massage is carried out during a facial treatment. Types of massage movements include effleurage and _____ techniques.

6. There are two basic types of _____, called setting and _____ masks. The effects of a mask depend on its ingredients, but it will generally have a deep _____ action on the skin.

7. A _____ is commonly applied to the face and neck at the end of a treatment. It helps to plump out the skin with moisture, which helps to reduce the appearance of fine lines. It may contain a _____ such as glycerine, which attracts water from the air and helps to prevent the product from drying out. It may also contain _____, which help to protect the skin from the damaging effects of the sun's _____ rays.

Facial terms word hunt

 ACTIVITY

Use the clues provided to find each hidden word. Shade in the boxes to show your answers. Remember: words can twist in all directions!

Type of mask that dries on the face

N	G	H	K
I	S	N	O
T	E	P	W
A	T	B	M

_____

Term that describes reddening of the skin

A	N	T	I
L	Y	H	P
A	E	R	C
M	U	K	E

_____

Product that helps to remove dead skin cells

D	R	O	P
I	A	T	E
W	I	F	X
C	L	O	P

_____

Product that removes dirt and grime from the skin's surface

Y	E	G	T
A	C	L	W
O	N	S	E
B	J	R	D

_____

Produced by the sebaceous gland and lubricates the epidermis

U	H	O	P
M	B	D	K
E	R	E	I
S	W	R	M

_____

A blackhead

P	E	D	O
M	B	N	G
W	O	E	S
A	I	C	Y

_____

Facial treatment

ACTIVITY

Shuffle the different stages of a facial treatment into the correct order.

❀ Apply a mask   1. _____

❀ Cleanse   2. _____

❀ Exfoliate   3. _____

❀ Massage   4. _____

❀ Moisturise   5. _____

❀ Remove eye make-up   6. _____

❀ Tone   7. _____

❀ Tone again   8. _____

Some basic facial treatments may only include a few of these steps but others may include treatments such as facial steaming.

Facial treatments crossword

  ACTIVITY

Answer the clues to complete the crossword.

Across

1. Redness of the skin (8)
7. A product used to remove any traces of excess grease from the skin (5)
11. A process of looking at the skin to determine the skin type and its condition (4, 8)
12. This product helps to plump out the skin and reduce the appearance of fine lines (11)
13. Applied to the face and neck in a thin layer and allowed to dry out (4)
14. Medium which can be used for facial massage (3)
16. With this skin type there will be areas of dry, normal and greasy skin (11)
17. These structures give the skin its strength (8)

Down

2. The feel of the surface of the skin (7)
3. A type of massage movement (10)
4. Product which helps to get rid of dead skin cells (10)
5. Usually consists of water and oil and helps to get rid of grease and dirt from the skin's surface (8)
6. The layer found below the epidermis (6)
8. Sebum and sweat mix together on the skin to form this (4, 6)
9. The shedding of dead skin cells (12)
10. This is found within the strongest toners (7)
15. The top layer of the epidermis (5)

Facial treatment procedures and their functions

ACTIVITY

Complete the following table.

Action/treatment	Why is it carried out?
Consultation	
Skin inspection	
Cleanse and tone	
Exfoliation	
Steaming	
Comedone (blackhead) extraction	
Massage	
Mask application	
Moisturise	

Aftercare advice

  ## ACTIVITY

In small groups, answer the following questions regarding aftercare advice:

1. Why do you give a client aftercare advice?
2. What aftercare advice is given?
3. How often should a client return for treatment?

1.

2.

3.

Contra-actions

  ## ACTIVITY

Think about possible contra-actions to facial treatment and how you would deal with an **adverse reaction**. Briefly discuss how you would recognise an allergic reaction.

key term

Adverse reaction an unwanted reaction that occurs during or after the treatment.

Your questions answered ...

Why do we complete the facial by applying moisturiser?

Applying moisturiser to the face is commonly the last step of the facial, as it helps to create a barrier between the skin and its environment, therefore protecting the skin from sun, wind, cold and air pollution. Moisturisers are mostly made up of water and oil. The water helps to put moisture back into the skin and the oil helps to stop loss of moisture from the surface of the skin. A moisturiser helps to plump out the skin with moisture, which helps to reduce the appearance of fine lines. It also helps to improve the feel (texture) and look of the skin as it softens it. Many moisturisers contain SPF (sun protection factor) to help protect the skin from the damaging effects of the sun's ultraviolet rays.

QUICK QUIZ

1. Which of the following is not a layer of the epidermis?
   a. Horny/stratum corneum
   b. Granular/stratum granulosum
   c. Adipose/stratum fatiosum
   d. Basal/stratum germinativum

2. Which of the following structures produces sebum?
   a. Eccrine gland
   b. Arrector pili gland
   c. Follicle
   d. Sebaceous gland

3. Which of the following skin conditions is infectious?
   a. Psoriasis
   b. Cold sore
   c. Eczema
   d. Acne vulgaris

4. What skin type is easily irritated by products?
   a. Dry
   b. Combination
   c. Oily
   d. Sensitive

5. Which of the following items would not be required to carry out a facial treatment?
   a. Buffer
   b. Toner
   c. Mask brush
   d. Moisturiser

6. Some toners produce a tightening effect on the skin, which is known as …
   a. Setting effect
   b. An astringent effect
   c. Hardening effect
   d. A humectant effect

7. Which of the following correctly describes a setting mask?
   a. A mask that is applied thickly onto the skin and left for an hour
   b. A mask that is applied in a thin layer and allowed to dry out

c. A mask that consists of ready-prepared substances, such as cream and oil
   d. A mask that requires heat to help it set

8. Which of the following is not a benefit of receiving a mask treatment?
   a. Improves the blood circulation
   b. Deeply cleanses the skin
   c. Helps to protect the skin from harmful sun rays
   d. Removes dead skin cells

9. Which product can be applied immediately after a facial treatment?
   a. Bronzing powder
   b. Mascara
   c. Foundation
   d. Blusher

10. Which of the following is a benefit of using moisturiser?
    a. Helps to add moisture to the skin, which helps to reduce the appearance of fine lines
    b. Exfoliates the skin
    c. Deeply cleanses the skin
    d. Has an astringent effect on the skin

11. Which of the following is not a cause of prematurely ageing skin?
    a. UV rays
    b. Drinking lots of water
    c. Smoking
    d. Rough handling of the skin

12. Which of the following aftercare advice would be given to a client after a facial treatment?
    a. Exfoliate the skin twice each day
    b. Use a product with an SPF (sun protection factor) of at least 5
    c. Have a facial treatment at a salon once a year
    d. Cleanse, tone and moisturise the skin twice each day

61

Working hygienically

 ACTIVITY

How would you clean or deal with the following items to ensure hygienic and safe working methods?

Brushes

Sponges

Used cotton wool

Palette

Used tissues

Eye pencil

Mascara

Lipstick

Germs can easily be transferred (known as **cross-infection**), so it is very important to ensure that everything is clean before use. Disposable items are ideal as they can be thrown away after use.

Allergic reaction

ACTIVITY

Describe what is meant by sensitivity testing (carrying out an allergy test).

Frontal
Parietal
Temporal
Nasal
Sphenoid
Ethmoid
Lacrimal
Zygomatic
Occipital
Maxilla
Mandible
Vomer

Bones of the face

ACTIVITY

Label this bone diagram of the face. If necessary, use books and the internet to help you.

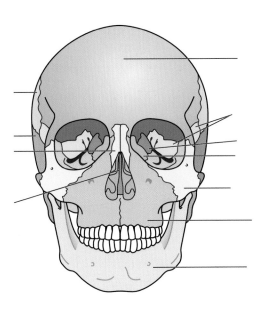

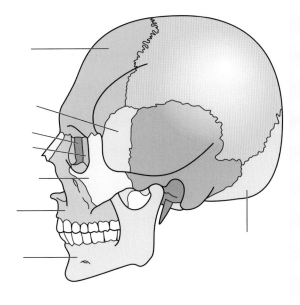

Muscles of the face

ACTIVITY

Label the diagram showing the muscles of the face using the list opposite. You can use books or the internet to help you.

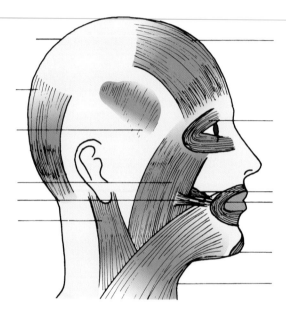

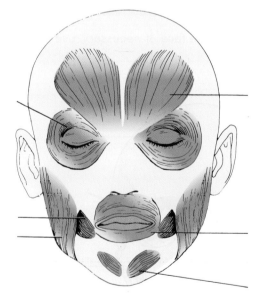

Frontalis	Masseter	Temporalis
Corrugator	Orbicularis oculi	Sterno-cleidomastoid
Buccinator	Mentalis	Platysma
Risorius	Orbicularis oris	Occipitalis

Client record card

ACTIVITY

Think about questions that you could ask to help you fully understand your client's needs so that you can provide an excellent make-up treatment.

Record all this information on a client record card, including your recommendations, so that you can refer to them at the end of the treatment. Discussing this information and any recommendations made will help you to sell retail products. Make sure that you escort your client to the reception area so that you can help with the purchase of any products that you have recommended. Also ask whether he or she would like to make another appointment.

Preparing for treatment

key term

Commercial time
a beauty treatment
needs to be carried
out within a certain
amount of time
to ensure that
the treatment is
profitable.

ACTIVITY

Complete the table by discussing each type of make-up service and the acceptable **commercial time** for each.

Type of make-up service	What is it?	Time to book out on appointment page
Special occasion make-up		
Bridal make-up		
Evening make-up		
Make-up lesson		

Bridal magazines will show bridal make-ups and will give make-up advice too.

ACTIVITY

Which of the following items would be required for make-up treatment? Draw the items onto the trolley.

Cleanser

Eyelash tint

Toner

Mask

Wax strip

Eyeshadow

Lipstick

Hoof stick

Moisturiser

Lipstick

Blusher

Blusher brush

Massage oil

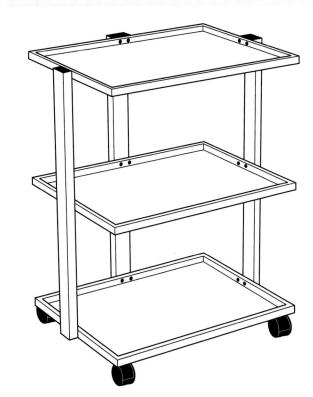

It is important that you have all make-up products and tools laid out neatly in preparation for make-up treatment. Time can be wasted if the beauty therapist has to search for missing items.

Can you think of any other items required for a make-up treatment? If so, draw them onto the trolley.

Contraindications to make-up

ACTIVITY

List the contraindications to make-up treatment.

Never tell a client that they may have an infectious disease. If the client has, for instance, a cold sore, even though you can't work directly over it you can apply make-up around it. A client can have a full treatment when they no longer suffer with a contraindication.

Contra-actions of make-up

ACTIVITY

Discuss any contra-actions to make-up treatment and describe how you would deal with the situation. Discuss how you would recognise an allergic reaction.

Make-up procedure

ACTIVITY

Put the following into the correct order.

❀ Apply blusher/bronzing products.

❀ Apply concealer.

❀ Apply eyebrow pencil.

❀ Apply eyeliner.

❀ Apply eyeshadow.

❀ Apply face powder.

❀ Apply foundation.

❀ Apply lip liner.

❀ Apply lipstick.

❀ Apply mascara.

❀ Use powder products to contour the face.

❀ Use powder to set lipstick.

1. _____

2. _____

3. _____

4. _____

5. _____

6. _____

7. _____

8. _____

9. _____

10. _____

11. _____

12. _____

Be aware that some make-up artists may follow a slightly different procedure when applying make-up.

Foundation

ACTIVITY

List five types of foundation.

1.

2.

3.

4.

5.

Foundation uses

ACTIVITY

Research five benefits of using foundation.

1.

2.

3.

4.

5.

Face powder

ACTIVITY

State four benefits of using a face powder.

1.

2.

3.

4.

Concealer

 ### ACTIVITY

Discuss the various types of concealers and their purpose.

Cream concealer

Liquids

Stick concealers

Medicated sticks

Corrective colour concealer

THINK

ACTIVITY

Match the corrective concealer to its description.

Green	Helps to conceal blue veins and pigmentation
Lilac/pink	Helps to hide dark rings under the eyes
Peach	Helps to brighten a sallow (yellowy) skin colour
Yellow	Used to hide redness on the face

Concealers containing pigment are useful for helping to even out skin colour on the face.

What make-up product am I?

ACTIVITY

A You put me on top of foundation and I often contain talc.

B I can be used to cover small **blemishes**.

C I can be used to make the eyelashes look longer and thicker.

D I help to make certain features of the face more noticeable.

E I can help make the lips appear slightly thicker.

F I help to draw attention to the cheekbones.

F I help to lessen the appearance of certain features of the face.

G I help to bring out the eye colour and come in many colours.

Make-up brushes

ACTIVITY

In small groups, research the features and uses of the following make-up brushes.

Blusher brush

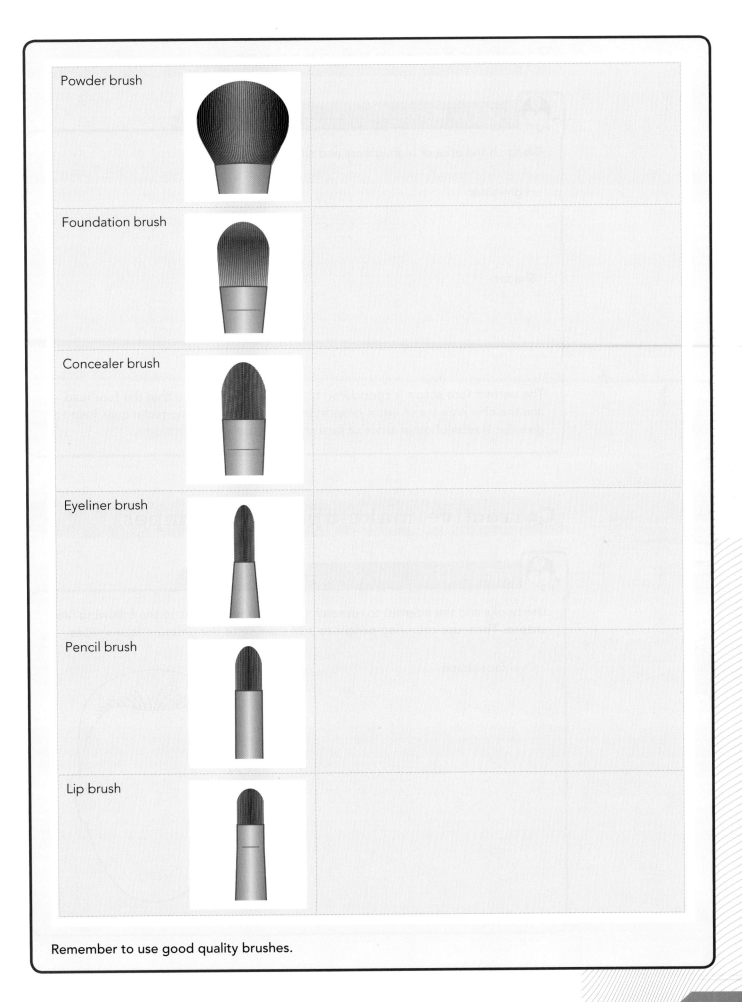

Powder brush

Foundation brush

Concealer brush

Eyeliner brush

Pencil brush

Lip brush

Remember to use good quality brushes.

Highlighters and shaders

ACTIVITY

Research the uses of highlighters and shaders.

Highlighter

Shader

The perfect face shape is considered to be oval, which means that the forehead and the chin area are of equal proportion. Corrective make-up techniques help to give the illusion of other kinds of face shapes as being oval in shape.

Corrective make-up to face shapes

ACTIVITY

Use books and the internet to research corrective techniques to the following face shapes. Then, use colouring pencils to add shading to the different face shapes.

Oval face shape

Round face shape

Square face shape

Long/oblong face shape

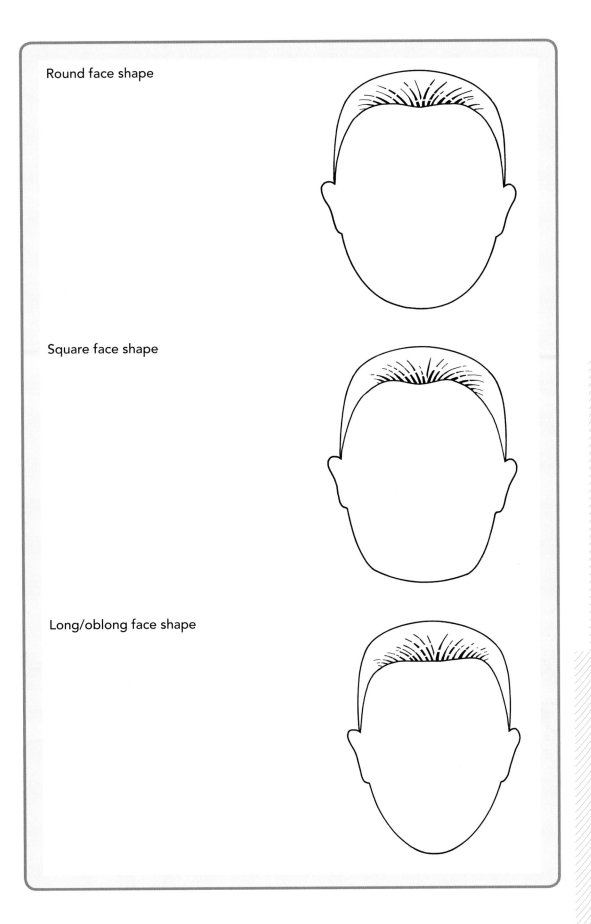

Heart face shape

Diamond face shape

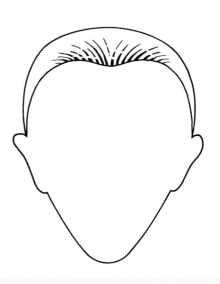

Corrective techniques for the nose

 ACTIVITY

Use books and the internet to research how you would carry out corrective techniques to the nose. Use colouring pencils to carry out corrective techniques to the various noses.

Long nose

Short nose

Thin nose

Wide nose

Large or protruding nose

Eyeliners

ACTIVITY

Match each type of eyeliner to their correct description.

Pencil

> This type of eyeliner is commonly contained in a bottle with a small brush. It may require some practice to become good at applying it but will give the eyes a more dramatic effect than the pencil, and does not smudge so easily. It is usually waterproof and is available in many colours.

Liquid

> This eyeliner may come in solid form inside a compact or container. It can be applied onto the eyes by dipping the eyeliner brush in some water and then applying some of the eyeliner onto the lids.

Cake

> This eyeliner is traditional in the Middle and Far East, including Egypt and India going back to the Bronze Age. It is easy to apply and glides on easily. It commonly includes iron oxide.

Kohl

> This is the most common type of eyeliner and is the easiest to use. It looks like an ordinary pencil and can be sharpened with an eyeliner sharpener. Some are encased in plastic tubes and don't require sharpening.

Corrective techniques for eye shapes

ACTIVITY

Use coloured pencils to help demonstrate how to apply eyeshadow to various shaped eyes. Briefly discuss the corrective techniques.

Small eyes

Prominent eyes

Round eyes

Deep-set eyes

Close-set eyes

Wide-set eyes

Droopy eyes

Blusher

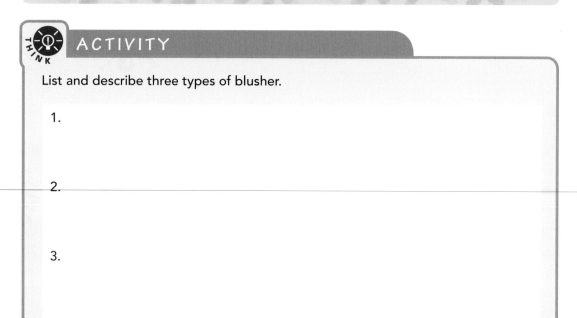

ACTIVITY

List and describe three types of blusher.

1.

2.

3.

Make-up treatment – fill in the gaps

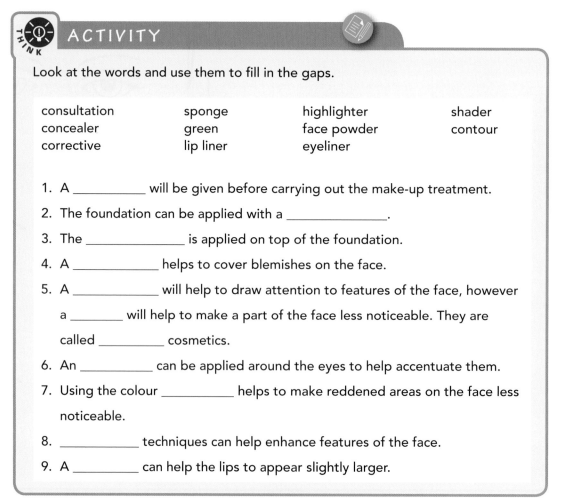

ACTIVITY

Look at the words and use them to fill in the gaps.

consultation	sponge	highlighter	shader
concealer	green	face powder	contour
corrective	lip liner	eyeliner	

1. A _____ will be given before carrying out the make-up treatment.

2. The foundation can be applied with a _____.

3. The _____ is applied on top of the foundation.

4. A _____ helps to cover blemishes on the face.

5. A _____ will help to draw attention to features of the face, however a _____ will help to make a part of the face less noticeable. They are called _____ cosmetics.

6. An _____ can be applied around the eyes to help accentuate them.

7. Using the colour _____ helps to make reddened areas on the face less noticeable.

8. _____ techniques can help enhance features of the face.

9. A _____ can help the lips to appear slightly larger.

Make-up treatment crossword

ACTIVITY

Answer the clues to complete the crossword.

Across

5. Usually made of plastic and used to store make-up products such as eyeshadows while carrying out a make-up treatment (8)
6. Helps to create an even skin tone to give a flawless finish (10)
7. Type of face powder (7)
9. A term used to describe a product which is unlikely to cause an allergic reaction (14)
13. Helps to draw attention to the eyes (8)
14. Passing infection either by direct contact, such as person to person, or by indirect contact such as dirty make-up tools (5, 9)

Down

1. A viral infection that is commonly seen around the mouth (4, 4)
2. Tools can be sanitised and stored inside this machine (5, 13)
3. Used to hide flaws, such as blemishes, on the skin (9)
4. Does not cause blocked pores or blackheads (3, 11)
8. A contouring cosmetic (6)
10. Type of blusher (6)
11. To make hygienic (8)
12. This colour is used to hide redness on the face (5)

Corrective lip make-up

ACTIVITY

Use books and the internet to research corrective make-up to different shaped lips. Use colouring pencils to demonstrate corrective techniques to the different lip shapes.

Thin lips

Full or thick lips

Uneven lips

Droopy mouth

Narrow mouth

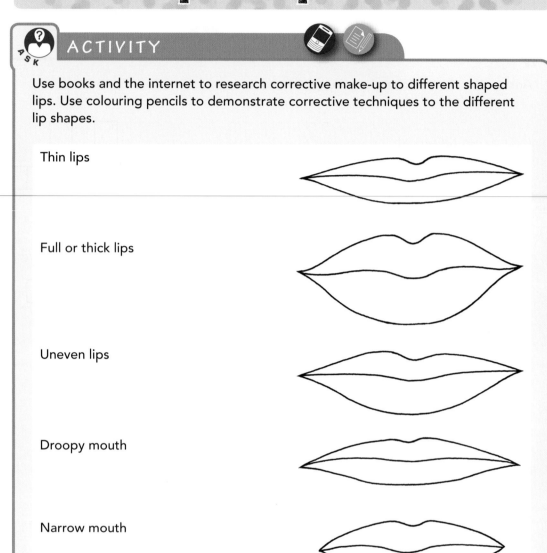

Aftercare advice

ACTIVITY

List the aftercare advice for make-up treatment.

Your questions answered ...

How do lip plumpers work?

Products are available that make the lips appear thicker. These products may produce a slight tingle and can be worn alone or under or over lipstick. They work by absorbing moisture from the skin. Some lip plumpers contain microspheres, which are tiny molecules often made from dehydrated marine collagen (dried fish). Others also contain a gel-like substance called hyaluronic acid. Ingredients effective in producing instant plumping and increasing the natural colour of lips include cinnamon oil, capsaicin (the spicy chemical in chilli peppers) and ginger; these substances irritate the sensitive skin of the lips and therefore stimulate the blood circulation so create more fullness.

Research the internet for different types of lip plumpers.

QUICK QUIZ

HOW MUCH DO YOU KNOW ABOUT ASSISTING WITH DAY MAKE-UP?

1. Which of the following is not required for make-up treatment?
   a. Tissues
   b. Highlighter
   c. Exfoliator
   d. Blusher

2. Which of the following cosmetic ingredients are known to cause allergies?
   a. Lanolin
   b. Parabens
   c. Perfume
   d. All of the above

3. At what stage of the make-up treatment would you generally apply lipstick?
   a. At the beginning of the make-up procedure
   b. After applying the eyeshadow
   c. Before the application of a concealer
   d. Toward the end of the treatment

4. Which colour would you use to conceal red broken capillaries?
   a. Green
   b. Lilac
   c. Peach
   d. Yellow

5. Which of the following is not a contour cosmetic?
   a. Highlighter
   b. Eyeshadow
   c. Shader
   d. Blusher

6. Which of the following describes a square face shape?
   a. A wide forehead and a narrow, pointed chin
   b. A narrow forehead and chin, and has the greatest width across the cheek bones
   c. A wide forehead and square jaw line
   d. A face with greater length in proportion to its width

7. If a nose is broad, where should you apply shader?
   a. To the tip of the nose
   b. To the sides of the nose
   c. To the bridge of the nose
   d. All of the above

8. What is a highlighter?
   a. A product that draws attention to, and emphasises, features
   b. A moisturiser that contains pigment
   c. A make-up product that adds intense colour to the eyes
   d. A cosmetic used to set foundation

9. Which of the following is not a type of mascara?
   a. Liquid
   b. Cream
   c. Milk
   d. Block

10. Which of the following is found in lipstick?
    a. Wax
    b. Oils
    c. Pigment
    d. All of the above

UNIT G2
Salon reception duties

This unit is about helping with salon reception duties. You will have to show that you can keep the reception area neat and tidy, greet people entering the salon, deal with their questions and make straightforward appointments. Using good communication skills when people come into, or telephone, the salon is a very important part of this unit.

You will need to be able to:
- ❀ maintain the reception area
- ❀ greet clients and deal with enquiries
- ❀ help to make appointments for salon services
- ❀ understand salon and legal requirements
- ❀ understand methods of communication
- ❀ understand salon services, products and pricing.

Key knowledge

✿ Laws relating to working as a receptionist
✿ Which items are required at the reception area
✿ How to greet clients face to face and by telephone
✿ How to deal with any enquiries from clients
✿ How to make appointments
✿ Abbreviations for treatments
✿ Understanding of body language
✿ The range of beauty treatments offered in a salon
✿ The types of products offered for sale in salons
✿ Methods of payment

What a reception!

 ACTIVITY

There are at least 10 reasons why you would not want to return to this salon – and they are all evident in reception!

Identify 10 things that are wrong, explain why they are wrong and, if there are any potential legal problems, state what they are in the table on the next page. Include the name of the relevant Act or the legislation (law) in the space provided.

What is wrong?	Why is it wrong?	Is it breaking any laws? If so, which laws?
1.		
2.		
3.		
4.		
5.		
6.		
7.		
8.		
9.		
10.		

The reception area is very important as it is usually the first part of the salon a client sees. First impressions count!

Reception duties

 ACTIVITY

List ten duties that a receptionist will be expected to carry out.

1.
2.
3.
4.
5.
6.
7.
8.
9.
10.

The receptionist is usually the first person a client will speak to in a salon. It is essential that the receptionist provides a good service as this helps to project a professional image for the salon as a whole.

Fake banknotes

ACTIVITY

Discuss five checks you can make to ensure that a banknote is not fake.

1.

2.

3.

4.

5.

If you have a bank note, look at it and check that it's real.

Cheques

ACTIVITY

Which of the following must the front of a cheque contain? (Tick the correct answers.)

- ☐ Client's signature (check that it matches the one on the card)
- ☐ Client's telephone number
- ☐ Correct amount in both words and numbers
- ☐ Correct date
- ☐ Name of the salon
- ☐ Name of the treatment
- ☐ Password details
- ☐ Time of the treatment

The number of the cheque guarantee card must be written on the back of the cheque by the receptionist, and the date on the card must be checked to ensure that it hasn't expired. If clients do not have a cheque guarantee card, they may not have enough money in the bank to pay what they owe to the salon. If this happens, the cheque will 'bounce' and the salon will not receive any money.

Managing appointments

ACTIVITY

Book the following clients onto the appointment page.

10.30 Mrs Hart – Eyelash tint and eyebrow shape, pedicure treatment Tel: 602876 (Charlotte)

9.30 Mrs Smith – Full leg and bikini-line wax, facial treatment Tel: 675843 (Sienna)

9.45 Mrs James – Manicure and pedicure Tel: 654967 (Madeline)

11.15 Mr Bedale – Facial and manicure Tel: 645312 (Jayne)

2.45 Miss Powell – Eyelash perm and body massage Tel: 680545 (Charlotte)

1.15 Miss Lucas – Nail extensions Tel: 564870 (Sienna)

2.15 Mrs Thould – Underarm, bikini and lip and chin wax Tel: 634869 (Madeline)

2.30 Ms Ward – Individual lashes and half-leg wax Tel: 875905 (Jayne)

The Beauty Place	Salon Appointments		Day:	Date:
	Charlotte	Sienna	Madeline	Jayne
9.00				
9.15				
9.30				
9.45				
10.00				
10.15				
10.30				
10.45				
11.00				
11.15				
11.30				
11.45				
12.00				
12.15				
12.30				
12.45				
1.00				
1.15				
1.30				
1.45				
2.00				
2.15				
2.30				
2.45				
3.00				
3.15				
3.30				
3.45				
4.00				
4.15				

Appointment booking mistakes

ACTIVITY

Look at the appointment page. It shows various clients booked in for treatments.
Can you find 10 mistakes? Write them in the space below.

	Jayne	Charlotte	Jess	Eve
9.00				
9.15	Mrs Jones			
9.30	EBS	F. leg wax		
9.45	////////	Tel: 604355		
10.00	////////			
10.15				Mrs Cott
10.30				pedicure and
10.45				manicure
11.00		Ms James	Peter	9732896
11.15	Mrs Taylor	Tel: 601966	Tel: 393460	
11.30	Luxury facial	Make-up, facial and	////////	
11.45	and lip and chin	nail extensions	////////	
12.00	wax		////////	
12.15	////////		////////	
12.30	////////		////////	
12.45	////////			
1.00	////////			
1.15		LUNCH	LUNCH	
1.30				
1.45		Ms Lucas		LUNCH
2.00		ELT		
2.15	LUNCH	no test		
2.30		given		Carol
2.45		9569273		Tel: 963975
3.00		////////		F. leg wax
3.15			Ms Willetts	U/A and
3.30			F. leg	bikini wax
3.45			wax	
4.00	Michelle		up/chin	
4.15	9657293		wax	
4.30	Nail extension and		sunbed	
4.45	F. body massage			

1.
2.
3.
4.
5.
6.
7.
8.
9.
10.

Reception wordsearch

ACTIVITY

Find the following terms in the wordsearch below. If you do not understand the terms, go back through the unit and find out what they mean.

F	K	C	K	O	T	E	M	A	E	N	D	M	L	Y	T	G
I	M	E	S	S	A	G	E	P	A	D	D	E	T	A	L	A
R	C	S	C	H	E	Q	U	E	C	C	U	N	P	L	P	U
S	D	H	T	S	A	D	A	C	O	L	E	T	E	P	E	L
T	S	C	R	O	N	D	N	U	C	I	N	I	O	S	T	P
A	T	D	E	N	C	G	A	O	L	E	C	I	I	I	C	L
I	C	R	H	A	I	K	T	C	I	N	N	D	C	D	N	A
D	R	A	C	D	R	O	C	E	R	T	N	E	I	L	C	H
K	E	C	U	C	R	I	P	O	M	D	P	P	I	I	S	L
I	D	Y	O	C	R	M	N	E	N	A	E	E	T	A	N	R
T	I	T	V	M	R	L	N	P	P	T	G	P	C	T	E	O
E	T	L	T	D	N	T	L	N	T	A	R	T	P	E	R	D
T	C	A	F	E	E	H	P	Y	I	B	C	O	A	R	R	R
I	A	Y	I	C	O	I	C	C	U	A	D	C	L	H	E	D
L	R	O	G	L	D	A	D	C	A	S	H	I	N	G	U	P
A	D	L	G	I	S	E	R	S	R	E	T	U	P	M	O	C
Q	E	N	O	H	P	E	L	E	T	I	S	E	Y	E	H	H

appointment	client record card	message pad
cash	computer	petty cash
cashing up	credit card	reception desk
cheque	first-aid kit	retail display
client	gift voucher	stock control
client database	loyalty card	telephone

Reception crossword

 ACTIVITY

Answer the clues to complete the crossword.

Across

1. Notes can be written onto this (7, 3)
8. Bank withdraws money from your bank account (5)
9. This should be given to a client after payment has been given (7)
11. Examples include eye contact and folding the arms (4, 8)
12. This can be kept at the reception in case of minor injury (5, 3, 3)
14. This treatment involves using a strip to remove hairs from the body (6)
15. A client may purchase one of these to give as a present (4, 7)

Down

2. Legislation which helps to protect client information (4, 10, 3)
3. Cards which contain client information (6)
4. A list which may be requested by a client (5)
5. This money is used to buy small items, such as a pint of milk (5, 4)
6. Type of electronic payment method (4, 3, 3)
7. A type of card which reminds the client of the time and date of their treatment (11)
10. A method of payment (6, 4)
13. This can be given to a client so they can test the product before buying it (6)

Body language

key term

Body language how people interpret the movements and gestures of a person's body, e.g. a slouched receptionist with folded arms may be interpreted as being unfriendly, bored and disinterested in dealing with the client. Positive body language with good eye contact sends the correct signals.

ACTIVITY

In the first column, list types of **body language** that you consider to be positive, helpful and friendly. In the other column, list body language that you consider to be unhelpful, unfriendly and negative.

Positive body language	Negative body language

Client communication

ACTIVITY

List four ways in which you can communicate with a client while working as a receptionist.

1.

2.

3.

4.

Telephone greeting

ACTIVITY

Write down the greeting that is given when a client telephones your salon.

Beauty treatments

ACTIVITY

Use the internet to research 10 beauty treatments that are unfamiliar to you. Discuss with other class members how long each treatment takes and what it involves.

Retail products

ACTIVITY

Research and describe six products that are commonly sold in salons.

1.

2.

3.

4.

5.

6.

Selling products to clients can be a good way to boost income for you and the salon.

Your questions answered ...

What should I do if a client insists they gave me £20 when they only gave me £10?

Inform the client tactfully that you believe it was £10 and that when the till is checked at the end of the day, if there is a discrepancy you will notify them. Make sure that you have the client's contact details.

When the client gives you a bank note, do not put it into the till until you have given change. This can save confusion if, for example, a client believes they have paid you £20 as you can show them the note they actually gave you.

QUICK QUIZ

1. Which of the following is least likely to be found at a reception area?
   a. An eraser
   b. Eyelash tint
   c. Appointment cards
   d. Wax heater

2. Which of the following is not a main duty of the receptionist?
   a. Making appointments
   b. Taking telephone messages
   c. Providing aftercare advice
   d. Providing gift vouchers

3. What is the recommended service time for a full leg-wax treatment?
   a. 10 minutes
   c. 45 minutes
   b. 25 minutes
   d. 1 hour

4. If the appointment page is set out in 15 minutes slots, how many slots would you book out for an hour treatment?
   a. One
   c. Three
   b. Two
   d. Four

5. What is a cash float?
   a. Cash paid for items such as milk and magazines
   b. Money that is put into a till at the beginning of the day or week to allow change to be given to customers
   c. A fake bank note
   d. The total amount of cash taken at the end of a working day and paid into a bank

6. What is petty cash?
   a. A small amount of money used to buy small items required by the salon such as milk and stamps
   b. A large amount of money kept in the safe and taken to the bank at the end of the day

   c. Money used to pay wages
   d. The change given to the client after paying for a treatment

7. What is a debit card?
   a. A card that allows a person to purchase goods and services by paying with money borrowed from a creditor. The borrower then repays the credit card company, often with interest
   b. A card which is issued by a retailer, with which a regular customer collects points that can be redeemed for discounts on future purchases, therefore the customer saves money
   c. A plastic card that provides an alternative payment method to cash when making purchases and removes money immediately from the purchaser's account
   d. A gift card purchased by a customer that may be given as a present

8. What is a PIN?
   a. Personal identification number
   b. Personal indication number
   c. Probable indemnity number
   d. Practical introduction number

9. Which of the following would be found on a debit card?
   a. Client's address
   b. Client's telephone number
   c. Client's date of birth
   d. Client's signature

10. Which of the following pieces of legislation is relevant to working in a salon?
    a. Health and Safety at Work Act 1974
    b. Supply of Goods and Services Act 1982
    c. Data Protection Act
    d. All of the above

UNIT N1
Assist with nail services

This unit is about assisting with, and carrying out, basic nail services on the hands and feet. You will need to be able to prepare for nail services by setting up the work area and using consultation techniques. You will also need to be able to carry out basic nail services, including filing, buffing, application of a suitable nail finish and hand and foot lotion. The service will also involve checking that the finished effect is to the satisfaction of a senior member of staff and the client. Advising the client on aftercare and leaving the work area in a suitable condition is also required.

To complete this unit, you will need to maintain effective health, safety and hygiene throughout your work. You will also need to maintain your personal appearance and good communication with the client.

You will need to be able to:
❀ use safe and effective working methods when assisting with nail services
❀ consult, plan and prepare for nail services
❀ carry out nail services
❀ understand the organisational and legal requirements related to nail services
❀ work safely and effectively when providing nail services
❀ Understand the contraindications and contra-actions of nail services
❀ use client consultation and service planning for nail services
❀ understand anatomy and physiology related to nail services
❀ understand the use of nail treatments
❀ provide aftercare advice for clients following nail services.

Key knowledge

- ❀ Laws relating to giving a manicure and pedicure treatment
- ❀ How to label a diagram of the nail and understand the function of each of the structures
- ❀ Common nail conditions and whether they are infectious
- ❀ How to work safely and effectively
- ❀ How to prepare a work area for nail treatment
- ❀ Which products are required for nail treatment and their uses
- ❀ Factors that can affect the nail's condition and appearance
- ❀ How to carry out a consultation with a client
- ❀ Familiarity with a consultation form and a treatment plan
- ❀ The differences between nail types
- ❀ Each step of the manicure and pedicure routine
- ❀ The different types of massage
- ❀ Aftercare advice and how often a client should return for further manicure and pedicure treatment

Structures of the nail

 ACTIVITY

Label the nail diagram.

| Free edge | Nail grooves | Nail plate | Nail walls |
| Cuticle | Nail bed | Lunula | Matrix |

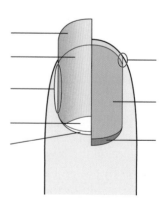

Which part of the nail am I?

ACTIVITY

Match each term to its correct definition below.

free edge	Tough part of the nail that protects the nail bed
nail grooves	Crescent shaped and mostly white in colour
nail plate	Cell division takes place here to form the nail plate
nail walls	Found at the side of the nails and act as guidelines for growing nails
cuticle	Extension of the nail plate that is cut and filed
nail bed	Overlapping skin found at the base of the nail
lunula	Folds of skin found at the side of the nails
matrix	Found under the nail plate and contains many nerves and **blood vessels**

Having knowledge of the nail's structures and their functions will help you to understand how the manicure and pedicure treatments affect and benefit them.

key term

Blood vessels tubes that carry blood around the body.

WATFORD LRC

Providing a safe and effective treatment

ACTIVITY

List 10 ways in which the therapist can ensure that a treatment is safe and effective.

1.

2.

3.

4.

5.

6.

7.

8.

9.

10.

Consultation form

ACTIVITY

In a small group, discuss what information is contained within a consultation from. Then make a list of 12 pieces of information that need to be included on a consultation form.

1.

2.

3.

4.

5.

6.

7.

8.

9.

10.

11.

12.

The consultation allows you to discuss what the treatment involves and also helps you to build a relationship with your client.

Devising a treatment plan

ACTIVITY

Devise treatment plans for the following nail conditions.

Dry and split nails

Minor corrugated furrows

It's important that the outcome of the treatment meets with the client's expectations, otherwise the client will not be pleased with the result and may not return to the salon.

Contraindications to manicures and pedicures

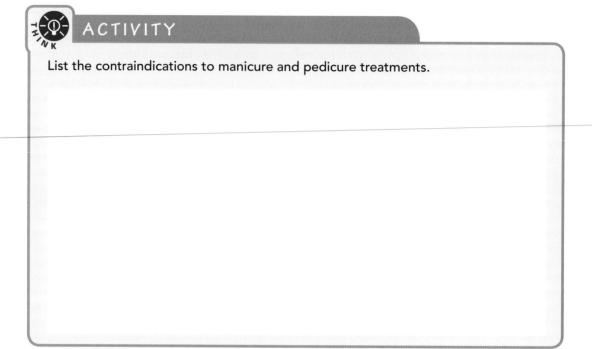

ACTIVITY

List the contraindications to manicure and pedicure treatments.

Nail conditions

ACTIVITY

List five treatable nail conditions and five non-treatable nail conditions.

Treatable nail conditions	Non-treatable nail conditions
1.	1.
2.	2.
3.	3.
4.	4.
5.	5.

Contra-actions to nail services

  ACTIVITY

Discuss and write down any contra-actions to nail services and how you would deal with them.

Manicure and pedicure equipment

 ACTIVITY

Study the list of tools and products below. Decide which are used during a manicure and pedicure treatment. Draw the items on to the trolley.

Wax pot
Tweezers
Foot file
Emery board
Record card
Individual lashes
Buffing paste
Buffer
Orange stick
Wax strip
Cuticle cream
Nail polish
Ear-piercing gun
Cuticle remover

The products, tools and equipment should always be neatly and attractively presented.

The use of nail treatments

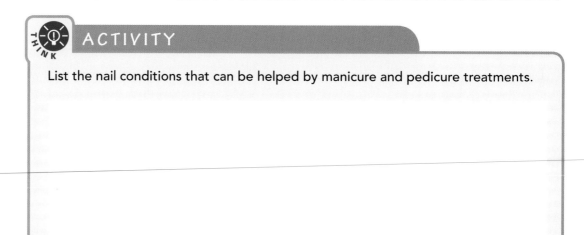

ACTIVITY

List the nail conditions that can be helped by manicure and pedicure treatments.

Manicure and pedicure procedures

ACTIVITY

Look at the list of words below and use them to fill in the gaps.

French manicure   acetone   bevelling   petrissage
ridge fillers   basecoat   cuticle cream   buffing
emery board   cuticle remover

1. Nail polish remover often contains _____ , which dissolves the polish. It is not contained within nail polish removers that are used for nail extensions.

2. Filing with an _____ will help to prevent splitting and breakage of the nails. _____ is a term used to describe the removal of roughness from the free edge of the nail.

3. _____ the nails with buffing paste helps to improve the circulation, which will help to improve the health of the nails.

4. _____ is applied to the nails to help soften the cuticles so that they may be gently pushed back if required.

5. _____ helps to dissolve dead cuticle and skin around the nail. It must only be applied to the immediate area, otherwise irritation may occur.

6. The hand and lower arm are often massaged during a manicure treatment. Massage movements include effleurage and _____ techniques.

7. A _____ helps to prevent staining of the nails when using a coloured nail polish. Special basecoats known as _____ help to even out the surface of slightly ridged nails.

8. A _____ involves applying a white nail polish to the free edge of the nail and covering the nail in a light pink polish.

Manicure and pedicure crossword

 ACTIVITY

Answer the clues to complete the crossword.

Across

3. The advice given to a client after a treatment (8)
7. This item is used to help remove dead skin from the feet (8)
9. No top coat is required if this polish is used (9)
10. The part of the nail that is cut and filed (4, 4)
11. These are known as Beau's lines and may be caused by ill health (10, 7)
12. This may be used if nail polish becomes too thick (4, 6, 7)
14. A small piece of dead skin that has split away from the cuticle and nail wall (8)
15. Found underneath the nail plate, and is rich with nerves and blood vessels (4, 3)
16. Cells divide in this area to make the nail plate (6)
17. Helps to even out the surface of slightly ridged nails (5, 6)

Down

1. Build-up of hard skin often found on the palms and heels (8)
2. Consists of a gritty substance and is applied to the nails (7, 5)
4. A nail shape (6)
5. Varnish that is applied to the nails to make them stronger and help to prevent breakage (4, 12)
6. These ridges may appear down the length of the nails and often accompany the ageing process (12)
8. Wooden stick with a pointed end and a hoof end that is tipped with cotton wool (6, 5)
13. A fungal infection that can affect the nails (8)

Manicure and pedicure: what am I?

ACTIVITY

Read the statements below and work out which product each one is describing.

exfoliant

> I am used to soften the cuticles so that they may be gently pushed back if required.

basecoat

> I may or may not contain acetone. You can use cotton wool and apply me to the nail plate.

cuticle cream

> I contain a gritty substance and am applied to the nail plate. A buffer is used to help spread me across the nail.

top coat

> I help to break down and dissolve dead cuticle and skin around the nail. I should not be left on for too long or I could irritate the skin!

nail polish thinner

> I am applied before coloured nail polish to prevent staining of the nail plate. Sometimes I am a ridge filler and help to give the nails an even surface.

buffing paste

> I can be used to thin nail polish that has thickened.

cuticle remover

> I can be used to help rub away rough, hard skin to reveal smooth, fresh skin underneath.

nail strengthener

> I help to seal and protect coloured nail polish.

nail polish remover

> I am really useful for nails that are brittle and damaged because I help to strengthen, condition and protect them.

Remember to follow manufacturer's instructions when using, storing or disposing of any beauty products.

Manicure and pedicure treatment word hunt

ACTIVITY

Use the clues provided to find each hidden word. Shade in the boxes to show your answers. Remember: words can twist in all directions!

1. A type of manicure that involves applying a white tip and a pale translucent nail polish

Y	C	N	G
A	W	H	E
U	O	R	S
B	L	A	F

_____

2. An item used to sterilise tools such as scissors

W	S	I	A
C	O	U	D
L	T	E	K
A	V	N	B

_____

3. A type of massage movement

B	F	E	T
F	O	L	U
V	E	R	A
P	I	E	G

_____

4. An infectious fungal condition affecting the foot – it causes itching, flaking and cracking of the skin

J	I	T	A
T	E	L	H
E	S	O	U
F	O	B	T

_____

5. A small piece of dead skin that has split away from the cuticle and nail walls

T	N	A	I
G	H	A	L
M	N	F	S
Z	B	U	W

_____

Nail services four-in-a-row

ACTIVITY

This is a game that involves two or more players. The objective of the game is to complete a row of four boxes vertically, horizontally or diagonally. You will need to photocopy the two sheets.

The worksheet headed 'Nail services four-in-a-row (1)' should be placed in front of the players to act as a game board. The sheet headed 'Nail services four-in-a-row (2)' should be photocopied and cut into cards. All of the cards are shuffled and placed face down. Each player selects a card and reads it aloud. If the card holder answers the question correctly, he or she may place the card on the correct box on the game board. If a player answers incorrectly, he or she misses a turn. If a question has previously been answered correctly and the box is covered, the card holder misses a turn. The winner is the first person who completes a row of four vertically, horizontally or diagonally.

Nail services four-in-a-row (1)

Free edge	Ridge-filling basecoat	Cuticle cream/oil	Hoof stick
Buffing	Nail polish	Orange stick	Matrix
Filing	Manicure bowl	Massage	Scissors
Foot file	Hot oil treatment	Top coat	Buffing cream

Nail services four-in-a-row (2)

Part of the nail that is cut and filed	Helps to make ridges on nails less noticeable	Helps to soften the cuticles	This item is used to gently push back the softened cuticles.
Helps to smooth the nails and gives a slightly shiny finish	Types include matt and pearlised	This item is useful for applying products to the nails.	An area where the nail is made
Part of the manicure routine that helps to make the nails shorter and smoother	Fingers are soaked in this item.	A relaxing part of the manicure that involves using cream or oil	Used to cut the nails
Item used to help get rid of dead skin on the feet	A treatment to help dry nails	Applied on top of nail polish to give a shiny finish	Consists of a gritty substance and is applied to the nails

Aftercare advice

ACTIVITY

In small groups, discuss the aftercare advice to be given to clients including how often a client should return for treatment. List the aftercare advice in the space provided.

key terms

Jaundice yellowing of the skin and whites of the eyes.

Anaemia a decrease in the normal number of red blood cells and is often due to lack of iron in the diet. It causes tiredness and lack of energy.

Diabetes disease related to the pancreas and the hormone insulin.

Thyroid gland in the neck that produces hormones.

Your questions answered ...

Is it true that nail colour and condition may indicate poor health?

Nail conditions, changes or abnormalities are often the result of nutritional deficiencies or some specific conditions. However, never inform a client that they may be suffering with an illness because their nails are in poor condition.

White nail colour may be a sign of fungal growth or liver problems.

White dots on the nails may indicate a zinc (mineral) deficiency or slight injury to the nail.

Brown nail colour may indicate fungal growth or kidney disease.

Yellow nail colour could be due to **jaundice**, a lung condition or, of course, too much smoking!

Blue nails may indicate poor circulation or a heart or lung condition.

Pitted nails may indicate a skin disorder such as psoriasis or eczema.

Pale, brittle, ridged and concave nails may be a sign of **anaemia**.

Breaking and splitting of nails may be a sign of thyroid problems.

Nails that are half-white and half-pink may indicate a kidney disorder.

Nails with a yellowish tint and pink colouring at the base of the nail may be linked to **diabetes**.

Ridges on the nails may be linked to eczema or **thyroid** problems. Vertical ridges may indicate shock or trauma to the nail and horizontal ridges may be linked to a respiratory disorder.

Curved nails may indicate a respiratory disorder.

Again, <u>never</u> tell a client that they may be suffering with an illness because of the condition of their nails.

QUICK QUIZ

1. Which of the following does not make up the structure of the nail?
   a. Cuticle
   b. Matrix
   c. Cortex
   d. Nail bed

2. The area below the cuticle in which cells divide to make up the nail plate is called the …
   a. Eponychium
   b. Matrix
   c. Lunula
   d. Nail wall

3. Which of the following is not a typical nail shape?
   a. Triangle
   b. Oval
   c. Square
   d. Pointed

4. Which of the following is an infectious nail condition?
   a. Split nails
   b. Dry/flaky nails
   c. Ringworm
   d. Hangnails

5. How would a therapist recognise athlete's foot?
   a. Shows itself as small black dots on the foot
   b. Dry/flaking skin often found between the toes
   c. Hard skin that is found on the toes
   d. Bruising of the nails

6. Which of the following items would not be required to carry out a manicure treatment?
   a. Cuticle cream
   b. Nail file
   c. Buffing paste
   d. Foot file

7. Which of the following products help to prevent staining of the nail from nail polish?
   a. Nail strengthener
   b. Top coat
   c. Basecoat
   d. Ridge filler

8. Why is it important to allow each nail polish application to dry before applying another?
   a. Otherwise the nail polish may smudge
   b. Otherwise it will be applied too thickly
   c. Helps to bring out the nail polish colour
   d. The top coat will not spread evenly onto the nails

9. Why should the nails be free of oil when applying nail polish to them?
   a. It could make it difficult to remove the nail polish
   b. It may cause staining of the natural nail
   c. It may affect the colour of the nail polish
   d. It may create a barrier so that the nail polish will not stay on the nails

10. Why is it important to complete treatments in the stated time?
   a. To ensure that the therapist is not late for their next client
   b. So the staff can take their breaks on time
   c. So the client will know what time the treatment will finish
   d. All of the above

Glossary

Acetone
A colourless, flammable liquid that can dissolve nail polish and nail extensions.

Adverse reaction
An unwanted reaction of a client to a treatment, which may occur during or after the treatment.

Anaemia
A decrease in the normal number of red blood cells and is often due to lack of iron in the diet. It causes tiredness and lack of energy.

Aromatherapy
Treatment that involves using oils taken from various plants.

Barrier cream
A substance used to prevent eyelash tint from staining the skin, e.g. petroleum jelly.

Blood vessels
Tubes that carry blood around the body.

Blemishes
Imperfections on the skin such as a scar.

Body language
How people interpret the movements and gestures of a person's body, e.g. a slouched receptionist with folded arms may be interpreted as being unfriendly, bored and disinterested in dealing with the client. Positive body language with good eye contact sends the correct signals.

Code of ethics
Set of guidelines that help to ensure a beauty therapist behaves professionally while working with clients.

Colleague
A person you work with.

Contraindications
Reasons why a treatment may be restricted or cannot go ahead.

Commercial time
A beauty treatment needs to be carried out within a certain amount of time to ensure that the treatment is profitable.

Cross-infection
Passing infection either by direct contact, such as person to person, or by indirect contact such as contaminated make-up tools.

Diabetes
Disease related to the pancreas and the hormone insulin.

Effleurage
A French word meaning to stroke lightly.

Epilation
Removal of the whole hair from the skin, including the root.

Germs
Tiny organisms, such as bacteria, which are capable of causing illness.

Hangnails
A small, torn piece of skin near a fingernail or toenail, usually caused by dry skin.

Hazard
A situation that may be dangerous and has the potential to cause harm.

Infectious
Can pass from one person to another.

Jargon
Language that is used by a certain group of people, such as beauty therapists.

Jaundice
Yellowing of the skin and whites of the eyes.

Legally binding
An agreement that is enforceable in a court of law.

Legislation
A law or a body of laws.

Massage mediums
Substances used to carry out a massage.

Petrissage
A French word, meaning to knead.

Petty cash
A small amount of cash that is kept aside for small purchases such as a carton of milk.

Risk assessment
To observe any potential hazard that could result in, for example, injury, illness or a dangerous situation.

Sterilise
To kill all germs such as bacteria. A machine called an autoclave can be used to do this.

Stock control
To assess how much stock is used and what and how much needs to be ordered.

Sunscreen
A substance that helps protect the skin from the sun's harmful rays.

Tapotement
A French word, meaning to drum.

Thyroid
Gland in the neck that produces hormones.

Toxic
Something that can be harmful to health.

Vitamin D
A vitamin needed by the body to ensure strong and healthy bones.